jesus freak

feeding   healing   raising the dead

SARA MILES

JOSSEY-BASS
A Wiley Imprint
www.josseybass.com

Published by Jossey-Bass
A Wiley Imprint
989 Market Street, San Francisco, CA 94103-1741—www.josseybass.com

Readers should be aware that Internet Web sites offered as citations and/or sources for further information may have changed or disappeared between the time this was written and when it is read.

Unless otherwise marked, all scripture is from the New Revised Standard Version Bible, copyright 1989, Division of Christian Education of the National Council of the Churches of Christ in the United States of America. Used by permission. All rights reserved.

Jossey-Bass books and products are available through most bookstores. To contact Jossey-Bass directly call our Customer Care Department within the U.S. at 800-956-7739, outside the U.S. at 317-572-3986, or fax 317-572-4002.

Jossey-Bass also publishes its books in a variety of electronic formats. Some content that appears in print may not be available in electronic books.

Library of Congress Cataloging-in-Publication Data
Miles, Sara, date.
  Jesus freak : feeding, healing, raising the dead / Sara Miles.
    p. cm.
  ISBN 978-0-470-48166-0 (cloth)
  1. Miles, Sara, 1952- 2. Christian converts—United States—Biography. 3. Saint Gregory of Nyssa Episcopal Church (San Francisco, Calif.)—Biography. 4. Church work with the poor—California—San Francisco. 5. Food banks—California—San Francisco. 6. Christian life—Anglican authors. I. Title.
  BV4935.M525A3 2010
  283.092—dc22
  [B]
                                    2009043621

Printed in the United States of America
FIRST EDITION
HB Printing   10 9 8 7 6 5 4

contents

for Paul
my Boyfriend's boyfriend

Author Note

This book is a work of nonfiction. To protect privacy, some names have been changed, as well as a few identifying details.

I used letters, e-mails, and my own notes as well as memory to reconstruct events and conversations, compressing stories and chronology in some places; I regret the inevitable errors.

To review my reporting, I checked facts and quotes with participants. Still, what happened over the course of writing this book was frequently wilder than I was able to record.

introduction

Y ou're such a freakin' Jesus freak, Sara," Paul said. "I mean that in the nicest possible way, of course."

The two of us had been cooking for hours, preparing lunch for the volunteers at our church's food pantry. Paul Fromberg was my friend and the rector at St. Gregory's, where I was a part-time lay staff member; together we served in the beautiful, Byzantine-inflected liturgy on Sundays. But every Friday we turned the sanctuary around the altar into a free farmers' market, opening it to anyone who walked in the door, giving away literally tons of free groceries to as many as eight hundred hungry families.

The food pantry was led by a gruff ex-con with missing teeth, who organized a hardworking crew of nearly fifty volunteers, mostly misfits and oddballs who'd come to get food. The volunteers were generally poor, and often didn't get enough to eat during the week, so we liked to make this lunch into a big family meal, with a couple of courses and a home-baked dessert.

In the grimy, maddeningly small kitchen, Paul and I had been bickering and banging into each other, cursing the dull knives and the broken Cuisinart. Two of our hotel pans had gone missing, so I'd made the green chile enchiladas in an assortment of cake pans. We ran out of oil. Then the oven rack, which someone had jammed in backwards, fell out as Paul was removing a tray of saffron rice, which spilled everywhere, nearly scalding him.

All morning long our volunteers had been wandering in to talk, even as, with mounting irritation, I kept shooing them out. A couple of junkies were skulking around, trying, purely out of habit, to get over on us. A thin schizophrenic girl kept hovering, asking me for candles and matches and glasses of water. The sweet middle school Latino kid who'd been suspended for cutting class wanted to hang out and brag to Paul about his girlfriends, and his mother kept dragging him away. "Carlos, just do one thing useful today, OK?" she'd snap. Out on the floor, a pallet of potatoes had spilled in front of the icon of the Virgin Mary, and our whole argumentative cadre of head-injured men was quarreling with a group of developmentally disabled adults over the right way to set up the snack table. "When is lunch going to be ready?" asked the tenth anxious helper, sticking a head into the kitchen. "What's for lunch? Are we eating soon?"

But I'd interrupted Paul just as he was plating the enchiladas. A young man in a black windbreaker had come by, worried about his upcoming visit to his sister and asking for a blessing. "You just always want to put your hands on everybody," Paul grumbled to me, but he set down his dish towel and leaned close, praying as I rested my hands on the man's bent head. "Gracious God," Paul finished, "fill us with the power of Jesus, amen."

"Amen," I said brightly. "Now let's serve. Is there another pan of rice? Oh, I forgot to tell you, we're getting that bunch of kids from Downtown High School for lunch today, too, but I'm sure we'll have enough for everyone, or you can make more beans."

"Jesus freak," said Paul, under his breath.

What does it mean to be a Jesus freak? Or, more to the point, what would it mean to live as if you—and everyone around you—*were* Jesus, and filled with his power? To just take his teachings literally, go out the front door of your home, and act on them?

It's actually pretty straightforward, Jesus says. Heal the sick. Cast out demons. Cleanse the lepers. *You* give the people something to eat. *You* have the authority to forgive sins. Raise the dead.

Throughout the Gospels, as he roams through Palestine, these are the commissions Jesus repeatedly hands to the ordinary people around him. Each is a specific call to action, a task for his followers to carry out on the spot—and to repeat when he's gone. They don't always understand, but he insists. You can do this stuff, he tells them. Walk this way. Come and see, don't be afraid.

After he's murdered, the story goes that Jesus rises from the tomb and knocks around for a while on earth, surprising his friends. He shows up on the beach grilling fish for breakfast, appears in the guise of a stranger on the road, reveals himself at suppertime in the breaking of bread, even offers his wounds for a doubter to stick his hands in.

Then one night, Jesus walks through a wall and simply appears in a locked room where his terrified disciples have been hiding from the religious authorities. Their Messiah is dead, their movement crushed, their hopes shattered, and they're completely unprepared for the man to stand among them again.

"Peace be upon you," Jesus says, and shows them his still-bloody hands and side. And then, for the final time, he tells his followers what he's been telling them all along: that they, too, are children of God, and that they are to continue doing Jesus' work, "even greater deeds than mine."

And so he stands quietly among his cowardly friends and just breathes on them. "Receive the Holy Spirit," he says. "As the Father sent me, so I send you." He breathes on them again. "If you forgive the sins of any, they are forgiven."

That commission evokes the moment of creation, when the Spirit of God breathed over the waters. But this is a new creation: Jesus is breathing more life into humanity. He is handing over the greatest power of all: to forgive sins, to make peace, as he's forgiven the friends and strangers who've betrayed and killed him.

From this power, and from the practical acts of mercy he's given every human being the authority to undertake now—feeding, healing, casting out demons, cleansing the ritually unclean—resurrection itself springs.

Jesus has given us all the power to *be* Jesus.

I came late to Christianity, knocked upside down by a midlife conversion centered around a literal chunk of bread. The immediacy of my conversion experience left me perhaps freakily convinced of the presence of Jesus around me. I hadn't figured out a neat set of "beliefs," but discovered a force blowing uncontrollably through the world.

Eating Jesus cracked my world open and made me hunger to keep sharing food with other people. That desire took me to an altar, at St. Gregory of Nyssa Episcopal Church in San Francisco, where I helped break the bread for Holy Communion, then to a food pantry that I set up around the same altar, where we gave away free groceries to anyone who showed up. From all over the city, poor people started to come every Friday to the church—100, 200, 450, 800—and like me, some of them stayed. Soon they began to feed and take care of each other, then run things, then start other pantries. It was my first experience of discovering that regular people could do Jesus' work.

In the thrilling and difficult years after my first communion, I kept learning that my new Christian identity required me to act. Simply going to church offered no ethereal juju that would automatically turn me into a less smug and self-righteous person. Time and again, I was going to have to forgive people I was mad at, say I was sorry, be honest when I felt petty, and sit down to eat, as Jesus did, with my betrayers and enemies: the mad, the boring, and the merely unlikeable.

As I got pushed deeper into all these relationships, I started to suspect that the body of Christ was not a metaphor at all. "Because there's one bread," as St. Paul, another poleaxed convert, wrote in astonishment, "we who are many are one body, for we all partake of the one bread."

I found that hard to swallow. Couldn't I *choose* whom I wanted to be yoked together with for eternity? And it was nerve-wracking. Sooner or later, I was going to have to consider the possibility that feeding wasn't the only command Jesus intended his one body to take seriously. All of us were also expected to heal, forgive, and raise the dead—not in some lofty symbolic way, but right here.

And yet—on what many of my new church acquaintances insisted on calling, rather smarmily, my "faith journey"—I began to taste something, see something, touch something which suggested that Jesus' vision of what we could do was true.

"I know this sounds nuts," I said to an old friend, who'd been shocked at my conversion to a faith I'd mocked, and baffled by my sudden urge to give away pallets of lettuce and cereal. "But, uh, when we're all together at the Eucharist and at the food pantry, it's the same thing. Because Jesus is real."

I went to church a lot. I'd moved through panic at the mere idea of sitting in a room full of Christians to a passionate engagement with worship. I encountered the transcendent power of ancient technologies: fire and water and beeswax candles burning all night. I heard the beauty of the unadorned sounds that suffering men and women can call forth when they sing in harmony. Ignorant of Scripture, I began to let King David's laments, Ezekiel's rants, and Mark's wire-service reports of miracles wash over me. I knelt. I smeared ashes on my forehead. I ate the bread of heaven. And as I sunk deeper and deeper into the practice, I began to sense how, even in church, we could follow Jesus: moving from piety to passion, from habit to risk, from law to love.

I had companions, notably Paul Fromberg, a gay priest from Texas, who'd emerged from Fuller Seminary, failed heterosexual conversion therapies, and a closeted job at an Episcopal cathedral with his faith miraculously intact. He praised God aloud without irony, and kept a postcard of Jesus on his desk, next to the pictures of his husband and family. A big man with a big heart and a big brain, Paul steered me, more or less patiently, through Scripture, answering questions as we chopped and cooked. "Did you ever think you'd wind up here?" he'd tease, as I got him to translate a Greek word, or explain the history of the Reformation. "I mean, when you ate that first piece of bread, did you have any clue what you were getting into?"

I didn't exactly study the Bible—that great mongrelized library of stories, books, letters, songs, unfinished manuscripts, polemics, lists, and lost treasures. Rather, I swam in it. I couldn't read Scripture in order to single out one lesson with a beginning, a middle, and an end, or use it to fix a stable doctrine. But in the Bible, the Book of Common Prayer, and the hymns of many traditions, I discovered something of the spaciousness of God's meaning, and the wildness of God's sense of time.

And I found that Jesus does not, anywhere in the Gospels, spend too much time calling his people to have feelings, or ideas, or opinions. He calls us to act: *hear these words of mine, and act on them*. I started to help lead liturgies, then write liturgies, because I wanted to take the language I found in Christian worship and use it as a blueprint for action in the world. Together, Paul and I wrote versions of the prayer sung at the altar during communion: "Sustainer of the covenant," one said, "you choose what is despised to make us whole." Both of us really knew that, in our own flesh. Paul and I, in different ways, had each brought our stigmatized bodies and hungry hearts to church, and discovered that Jesus was waiting there, completely unbothered. As our grateful prayer said, "In the midst of our shame, you cover us with a garment of love."

St. Gregory's had given me room not only to receive but to give. And it allowed me to act as if the stuff we did on Sundays meant something, and was a guide to our whole lives, in church and outside.

Worship and service were parts of a whole; the Friday food pantry and the Sunday Eucharist were just different expressions of the same thing. Well-meaning Christian visitors liked to describe the pantry as a "feeding ministry," but that just seemed like a nervous euphemism to me. What I saw was church: hundreds of people gathering each week around an altar to share food and to thank God.

And then, on Sundays, in the very same space, communion. "In the fullness of time bring us," the congregation would sing, "'with every tribe and language and people and nation, to the feast prepared from the foundation of the world." The priest, and whoever else was serving that day—a woman with cancer; a fussy older guy; a serene, angelic seven-year-old boy in shorts—would lift the plates of fresh bread and cups of wine and turn, showing the food to the people standing pressed close around the big round table in the middle of the sanctuary. You never knew who'd be holding the bread. Paul liked to say that "the surest sign of Jesus' presence in the Eucharist is when there's somebody completely inappropriate at the altar."

Frequently that was me. "Jesus welcomes everyone to his Table," I'd announce, "so we offer the bread and wine which are Christ's body and blood to everyone, without exception." There was no altar rail or line, so we'd head out into the crowd, carrying communion to clergy and teenagers, old ladies, Jews and baptized Christians, random visitors. "The body of Christ," I'd say, looking each person in the eyes and handing each person Jesus. And time would stop, over and over and over.

This thing is real.

On Fridays at the food pantry, I'd get the same overwhelming sense of truth, of being part of something bigger than my own likes or dislikes or imagination. I watched the concrete, earthy body of Christ take form in pushy Chinese grandmothers, thieving heroin addicts, and weepy transsexuals who came to get food, then wound up feeding others. I watched myself, and the people around me, start to change.

"Coming here made the biggest difference in my life," admitted Blanca, one of the volunteers, when she told me how she wound up serving at the pantry. "I was newly sober. The world was raw to me, and I was raw to people." Her long soft hair was falling out of a bun, and she poked it back in place, looking at me intently. "In six years' working here I've learned to be a little more of a team player and less the big-mouth," Blanca said, quietly. "Now I yell but then say I'm sorry. We're learning to how be with each other."

Sharing food in this way was about making whole new lives possible. At the food pantry, we drank out of the same cups and put our sick, scarred hands on each other. We ate without washing correctly. And sometimes, when we thought were just going to have lunch, we tasted heaven.

None of it was easy. As one friend said, ruefully, when I complained about a filthy, hostile visitor to the pantry, whom I kept wanting to bounce: "Sara, if you want to see God, sometimes you have to sit in the smoking section." Or, as I wrote to a colleague, complaining about St. Gregory's parishioners: "The thing that sucks about being a Christian is that God actually lives in other people."

In church on Sundays, and at the food pantry on Fridays, I found myself overwhelmed by the implications of the incarnation—the inescapable physicality and humanity of a God who should have known better than to dwell in this muck with us. I craved the deepening meaning Jesus brought to my life. But to get there I had to get over myself.

I realized how my continuing conversion depended on being thrown together in intimate ways with all kinds of strangers I hadn't chosen. Being the body of Christ didn't allow a lot of room for sentimentality or waffling, and didn't depend on my ability or failure to like any particular individual. It just demanded a new heart from me, a new way of seeing other people.

They hugged me at the Peace on Sundays, when I wished to be left alone; they sang hymns irritatingly off-key until I turned around to glare, and then smiled at me. Or they showed up at the pantry after disappearing on two-month benders, cheerfully offering to share their stale sandwiches and beer; they gave me ripped-out pages from their secret journals, and flowers they'd stolen from the city park. One Friday a guy pulled down his shirt to show me his broken collarbone, where another angry meth-head had slammed him with a two-by-four. One Sunday while I was trying to get my sermon ready, a suburban mom held on to my hand for half an hour before she told me her daughter had tried to kill herself. Kids climbed on me, old ladies patted me, my priest delicately wiped a smear of chocolate pudding from my hair.

If Jesus is about anything, it's the inconvenient truth that a spiritual life is a physical life. The people I met were Jesus' body: suffering, feeding each other, healing the sick, forgiving one another, rising out of death. Their freaky hands and legs and backs were doing his work, carrying his power through the world.

It might be comforting, to those Christians who doubt the current indwelling of the Holy Spirit in our damaged, compromised selves, to tell ourselves that our failures are because Jesus is now far, far away.

It might be reassuring, to those tired of dealing with our violent, scary, or just unpleasant neighbors, to think that we can worship God by turning our backs on them. That we can't do much anymore about our lives, or the lives of other people, except gaze at the sky and pray to a disembodied spirit. That Jesus was alive once, and we remember him fondly, but now we're left with nothing more powerful than plastic crosses, Christian rock bands, and church committees. With Jesus safely tucked away in heaven, we're off the hook.

But he's still breathing in us.

I was standing at the bus stop across from the church one Friday, as the food pantry was winding down, talking with Miss Lola Brown. A tiny, elderly black lady with sensible shoes and bent, arthritic hands, she was shaking her head in despair because she didn't know how to get her groceries across town to her apartment. "I can't even *lift* this," she said, pointing to the teetering shopping cart, filled to overflowing with potatoes, cans of beans, and some exuberant heads of lettuce.

I was exasperated. I didn't have a car. I didn't have money to give her for a cab. I had to be somewhere else in a little while. I looked at the man standing next to us, a big, quite psychotic white guy, a ranter, who'd also just been at the pantry. "OK, we'll help you," I said, not very nicely. I had no idea how. And then the bus pulled up, and the man shuffled forward, muttering, and the two of us lugged her cart on board.

Miss Brown smiled and raised her hand to heaven. "I know," she testified. "I *know* the Lord will always send me help."

I told that to my wife, Martha, when I got home, and she rolled her eyes. "Couldn't the Lord send her a taxi at least, if he's got all that power to help?" she asked. "Instead of a crazy guy and some feeble middle-aged lady, and she's still got to take the 22 Fillmore for an hour?"

"Nah," I said. "Jesus has a sense of humor. He just sends us."

Like most people, I have an ambivalent relationship to power. I want it and I'm scared of it. I think I couldn't possibly use it well, and I know others can't. Why should humans receive the power of the Spirit? Isn't that what God's for?

But Jesus is right here with me and the crazy guy—the lowly and unprepared, as the prophets foretold. Among the weak, faithless, and doubting, as his disciples proved, then and now. He doesn't look for the most "religious," the most doctrinally correct, or, for that matter, the smartest of his beloved people to build his kingdom, but hands over authority to anyone willing to suspend self-doubt and simply trust Jesus' faith in us.

There is no other authority on earth we have to wait for, no permission we need in order to act on his words. All it takes to be a Jesus freak is to follow him.

come and see

Somebody told me a story. And it turned out to be true.

According to Jewish and Christian tradition, we understand God through stories. How the stars were set in the firmament. The time the big brother cheated the little brother. What happened to the women who went to the tomb and found it empty. The Bible is stuffed with tales that jumble together the stuff of spirit—burning bushes, angry angels, mysterious clouds, and voices from heaven—with the most prosaic and earthbound details: bread, water, a coat; bricks, weeds, an argument among siblings, labor pains. We can barely wrap our minds around it all, but we keep listening. By the time Jesus appears, he's holding everything indivisible: body and soul, heaven and earth.

I tasted Jesus before I read about him, and turned back to Scripture for clues about what I'd already experienced in my own body. Listening to and reading the Gospel accounts felt, for me, like the opposite of that old game of Telephone, where a phrase is passed down a line, losing its sense as each person attempts to repeat the words exactly. Instead, the tales about Jesus only gain significance in repetition, gain depth and breadth as they resound through different readers, are stuttered or proclaimed in a million different voices, down the years. Interpretations multiply, but in place of chaos there's a glimpse of something that looks like truth: vast as galaxies flung across a night sky, specific as a puddle by the side of a road in Galilee or a rutted sidewalk in East Oakland.

Here's what I hear: Jesus is the Word made flesh. While he lived among us, what he said and what he did were the same thing. His human body was God's language, as much as his human speech.

Sometimes, in the Gospels, this language is easy to read, as when Jesus lifts a hand to rebuke the waves; pronounces, "Be quiet"; and the tempest is stilled. Sometimes it's frustratingly mysterious, as when he scribbles in the dirt with a stick or invites his friends to eat his flesh. Jesus' dense parables are invitations into more and more meaning, as are the daily actions he undertakes: walking, washing, lifting, touching, sleeping, eating a piece of grilled fish with his bare hands.

But it's all teaching, and it's all driving toward a point—though it's frequently confusing. "What do you see?" Jesus asks, as he rubs spit in someone's eyes. Or, teaching a clueless crowd: "What do you think that landowner would do?" Then, in a seemingly unconnected gesture, he takes off his clothes, kneels down, and washes some man's feet.

But I don't think the words and the actions recorded in the Gospels are random. Jesus is showing his disciples

2

some crucial things about the nature of God, so that they could participate fully in God's work after he was gone. So that their feeding, healing, and forgiving would take place on God's terms, and add up to resurrection.

In stories that still have the power to scare us, Jesus tells his disciples to live by the upside-down values of God's kingdom, rather than the fear-driven values of human society. He shows how family, tribe, money, violence, and religion—the powers of the world—cannot stand against the love of God. And he tells us that we, too, are called to follow him in breaking down all worldly divisions that get in the way of carrying out his instructions. Sure, it's impossible to feed five thousand people, make a deaf man hear, bring a dead girl to life, as long as you obey human rules. So do it God's way instead, Jesus teaches. *Say yes. Jump right in. Come and see. Embrace the wrong people. Don't idolize religion. Have mercy.* Jesus' tips cast a light forward, steering us through the dark.

Say yes. This message is first delivered not by Jesus but by his mother, following her astonishing encounter with the angel Gabriel. "OK, God," Mary says to the impossible proposition, and Jesus comes to live in her.

As an unmarried girl in the ancient agricultural world, Mary represents the most unlikely spokesperson for a powerful deity. Yet this unimportant person fearlessly carries God's good news that the proud will be scattered in their conceit, the hungry will be filled with good things, the rich sent away empty, and the lowly lifted up.

It is, of course, profoundly unsettling news: Mary doesn't need a man to have a baby. She isn't going to follow worldly norms. In fact, she prophesizes the overturning of the whole social order. She doesn't ask permission of kings or family or priests to step off the precipice into unprecedented experience.

But her choice is also revolutionary because she submits. Mary sings out her *yes* without knowing what will happen. Trusting God, Mary opens herself to humiliation, physical pain, dislocation, terror, loss. And yet, just as Jesus will, she calls herself blessed.

Her courage remains a signpost for all humankind—for all the unimportant, frightened, powerless people who doubt that God can work through us. As the fourth-century bishop Gregory of Nyssa wrote, "What was achieved in the body of Mary will happen in the soul of everyone who receives the Word."

Reports keep showing up over the centuries of Mary speaking to people in their own languages, appearing to cripples and prisoners, to refugees and shame-filled pregnant girls, sharing the message that the angel brought her: *Don't be afraid.* She whispers that it doesn't matter how unqualified we think we are; God can make new life in us, too.

Because at the annunciation, Mary didn't get safety. She got a child she couldn't give a place to lay his head, a child she couldn't save from violence. Mary said *yes*; she got Jesus.

Jump right in. I like to think Jesus learned something about saying *yes* from his mom. In any case, he repeats the message at his baptism, driving home a few more essential points about the nature of God's relationship with humans.

The first thing we learn from the story of Jesus' baptism is that God is probably not planning to reveal anything particularly important in church, or in any kind of temple we think is appropriate for the holy, or through anyone who's an official holy man. It's nice to imagine John the Baptist as a revered religious leader who led beautiful spiritual ceremonies outdoors, in the lovely flowing water. But John the Baptist was, not to put too fine a point on it, a total nutcase, sort of like the unwashed guy with the skanky dreadlocks and the plastic bags over his socks who sleeps in the entryway to the library. John the Baptist ate bugs. He ranted and raved and spoke sedition. He railed at decent temple-goers, shouting that their sacred ceremonies were useless, threatening them with damnation if they didn't repent. And though he wasn't a priest, he dared to claim that he could baptize for the forgiveness of sins.

And the river Jordan was not even slightly picturesque: it was a muddy stream, right by the side of a public road, and John told people to walk into it, all kinds of men and women together, with no respect for order. The contemporary equivalent would be a homeless schizophrenic waving his fist at priests and cops, then yelling to a crowd that they should get down on their knees together on the filthy floor of the bathroom in the Greyhound bus station and repent.

In other words, just as the unmarried teenager Mary is the mother of God, so the madman John is the baptizer of God: both improper figures, completely unauthorized by the religious authorities. And just as a mucky feed trough is where Mary lays the bread of heaven, so the river Jordan is where John anoints the Son of God: inappropriate locations for something holy to occur.

This common water is where Jesus chooses to be baptized. This profane setting, outside the majestic temple doors, is where God chooses to reveal his love for his son. Like the table Jesus will share with tax collectors and sinners, like, in fact, the cross: these scandalous places are exactly where we will find salvation.

And then Jesus does nothing pious to please God. Jesus doesn't say the correct prayers first, or do good deeds, or offer animal sacrifice to win God's favor. He just *is*. He jumps into the river, the rushing water of the world, with his human body, and the Spirit of God comes over him. Jesus and God and the Spirit know each other, and God says: this is my son, my beloved, with whom I am well pleased.

This recognition, this total union among God and Jesus and the Spirit, tears the heavens. It rips them apart, just as they will be ripped apart at the crucifixion. The veil between heaven and earth, the veil constructed by religion to separate humans from God, is torn asunder forever by the absolute fact of Jesus. Jesus who is utterly, dirtily human; Jesus who just wades into the water and accepts the divine Spirit coming to dwell in his flesh. As it will, through him, come to dwell in us.

And how do we know this? *Come and see,* says Jesus, kicking off his public ministry after his baptism. It's a statement that's got more than a little dare in it; more than a little edge. This is the Jesus that Paul and I started referring to as "the Boyfriend." We used it as a colloquial version of the ancient Christian name of "Bridegroom" for Jesus, but it felt more personal—and funny, if a little disturbing, because that's how Jesus is.

In the Gospel story, Jesus asks two of John's disciples what they're looking for, and Andrew politely says, "Rabbi, where are you staying?" Then the Boyfriend says, simply, *come and see.* In this story we learn what Jesus is like, and how he sees us, and what he's going to ask of us, the disciples. How our relationship is going to be.

Right away, the Boyfriend makes clear where he's staying. He is staying with us. On earth. Period. And he's inviting us to come and see what it means to abide in a human body in the world. The Boyfriend is moving in.

So what's he like? One, he's promiscuous. Because Jesus is the kind of boyfriend who'll go with anyone. He picks up John's disciples. He chats with strangers. He'll even flirt with two brothers at the same time—he has no shame. Jesus talks to anyone: Jews, Gentiles, women, children, foreigners. He's soft on them. He touches them. He calls them by name.

Two, the Boyfriend is a bit of a troublemaker. He likes to stir things up. In the conventional order, only members of Aaron's royal family get anointed to the priesthood in an exclusive temple ritual. But Jesus goes to John, the mad prophet, instead. Jesus wades right in and comes up shining, and then he starts getting everyone else riled up. Okay, ready or not, he says, let's go: *come and see.*

Jesus isn't the kind of boyfriend, in my experience, who's just going to smile and be agreeable. He's the thrilling, scary Boyfriend who's going to dare you to do things you'd never dreamed of, shower you with unreasonable presents, and show up uninvited at the most embarrassing times. Then he's going to stick with you, refusing to take the hint when you don't answer his calls.

In the story of Andrew, Jesus is just beginning his love affair with all humankind. That first baptism in the Jordan will lead to baptisms of fire, tears, the cup, and the cross; Jesus will submit and go under it all, falling and coming up, dying and rising, and he will never, ever, let his lovers go.

But to start, Jesus simply looks at us. He sees us, face to face. And what he sees about us—his confused, doubting, selfish followers—is that we, too, are beloved children of

God. That we, dumb and dim as Andrew, as Peter, as any crushed-out ninth-grade girl or sulky teenage boy, are part of the Boyfriend's body: one flesh with him, and with all humankind.

Oh, my dears, says the Boyfriend. This is how it's going to be from now on. All those other discipleships are over, because I'm here now, for good. This is what our relationship is going to be like: I love you, and you love me and each other. *Come and see.*

Jesus doesn't make us obey by claiming the mantle of religious authority or worldly power: he meets us at someone's ordinary house, at four in the afternoon. He doesn't ask us to prepare and purify ourselves: he takes us as we are. This Boyfriend is not a big talker. He just invites us, without exception, into experience. It's a dare, and it's a promise. *Come and see,* he says. Our Boyfriend insists on staying with people. He abides with us in the lowliest places, kisses the most despised sinners, sticks around for the worst messes humans can make. And even when we doubt the love, even when we wreak jealous violence on his other beloveds, even when we try to break up, the Boyfriend is still there. He still wants us to touch him, eat him, become him.

Because the thing about Jesus, the story turns out, is that he believes in *us,* the people who betray his love, just as he believed in Andrew and poor frightened Peter. Jesus trusts that humans have the power to truly see him ourselves. He believes that our mortal bodies, our experiences here on earth, are enough to bear and hold

God. He knows we can find him in our own flesh, and in the flesh of others.

✠

Embrace the wrong people. In the public works that follow his baptism and call to those first followers, the itinerant teacher and healer Jesus keeps making the point that salvation doesn't depend on worldly status, or even on religious observance. In a whole series of stories, Jesus demonstrates that God deliberately chooses the stranger, the outcast, the foreigner, the sick and unclean—in short, the wrong people—to show the scope of his love.

The story of Jesus and the man blind from birth begins with the assumption—common to all cultures—that we can exclude people from the ranks of God's beloved. In this example, the blind man is assumed to be guilty: either he or his parents must have sinned to cause his defect. In other stories and other times, we see slaves, foreigners, cripples, the sick, sexual deviants, and beggars excluded, forced to fill the role of the sacrificial victim.

These victims are key to every human story, because outcasts define the center. It works the same way in our own time: you hear what you call an accent, and you know by this that you aren't a foreigner. You see a guy who acts like a fag, and you know you're a real man. You see the slow kids sitting by themselves in the junior high school lunchroom, and you know you're normal. And the church, of course, needs heretics in order to establish orthodoxy. So outcasts are essential, because they define the norm for the rest of the community.

And the laws of religion, then and now, thrive on our need for outcasts. They codify who's in and who's out, what's a right day for healing and what's a wrong one, who's pure and who deserves to be struck down with a disease that makes them untouchable. Then the priests, as Jesus knew well, become the only ones allowed to pronounce someone healed or contaminated, the only ones who can establish who's inside and outside. It's a system that the world—and religion—run well on.

But when Jesus restores the blind man's sight, he offers us a way to let God's radical grace disrupt this system. To live in faith. To see as God does.

It's a frightening offer, because accepting it means accepting that healing may not always come the way we wish it to. That the strange or the sick may, in fact, hold the key to the healing of the "normal" ones. That priests can't decide whom God loves.

None of us can control what God does. But we can open our eyes and see what God is doing. Jesus says that in order to see the glory of God revealed, we have to look at the whole of creation: God is always among us, making us whole even as we try to divide ourselves, loving us even as we hate each other.

Look at the lame, he says, at the plagued, the poor: those you've cast out, those whose suffering you misinterpret as a sign of their own sinfulness. Don't call unclean

11

anything God has created; do not exclude anything or anyone from your vision. It is all God's work.

✠

Then, in the story of the Samaritan woman, Jesus chooses to engage with a three-time outcast. She's female; she's a member of a despised, loathsome race, the historic enemies of the true people of God. And, to top it all off, she's five times married, and living with a man she isn't married to. The Samaritan woman is repugnant, not only to a Jew like Jesus but to her neighbors. She has to go alone to the well, because no decent person wants to be seen in her company.

But Jesus is thirsty. He asks for water. He offers her water that will slake her thirst forever.

And when the woman argues, claiming insolently that this is Jacob's well and that her traditions of worship are correct, he doesn't tell her she's wrong and his people are right. He says the Spirit of God isn't limited by tribe or ancestors or behavior; it's poured out for everyone. Then, without judgment, he tells her exactly who she is.

The Samaritan woman doesn't fully understand Jesus. She doesn't immediately accept the relationship he offers. Even when he tells her the truth, she tries to cling to her own received religious dogma.

But she really wants that water. "Give me some of that water," she demands of the strange rabbi. And her thirst leads her to bring others to the well—without telling them what to believe, just by echoing the great door-opening

Gospel invitation, *Come and see*. Jesus transforms this woman without a name, this despised status offender, and she becomes the first person to preach Jesus as Messiah. Which would seem to suggest that salvation does not depend on getting things right. It depends on thirst.

In yet another passage, Jesus, in a reckless, escalating display of passion, shows how his works depend on embracing every kind of wrong person. First he hangs out with some tax collectors—those despised collaborators with empire, the crooked cops of their day. He not only touches them but eats with them. In a world where eating was saturated with ritual, Jesus demonstrates, shockingly, that God's table isn't just for good people. It's for sinners and even the people who hurt you. It includes everyone, without exception.

Then, a bleeding woman: someone gross, literally untouchable, who could contaminate the otherwise pure merely by brushing against them. Jesus not only allows himself to be touched but puts his hands on her, and moreover calls her daughter. He proclaims: there is no religious distinction between clean and unclean. No human being is outside the family of God.

And then Jesus breaks the most powerful taboo and touches a dead body. The daughter of Jairus has died, and Jesus crosses the line that his religion has declared fundamental: the line between living bodies and corpses. And so he declares: God's love is forever and for everyone.

Even death can't hurt us, because God's mercy endures past physical death.

By physically showing mercy to the impure, to bad people, Jesus is healing not just the sinners and tax collectors, the bleeding woman and the dead girl. His embrace restores the entire community to wholeness, so that we can live indivisible, as the one human family God has made.

In the story of the man with a virulent skin disease, Jesus shows how God works by refusing to sacrifice human beings to rituals. The story, not technically of a healing but a cleansing, takes place in the context of the Levitical system of laws. These laws' purpose went beyond establishing practices of physical health for communities understandably terrified of contagious diseases. They were ritual ways for priests to discern, express, and bring about God's desired order for his people.

In the Levitical system, order comes by expelling the disordered one. The community is kept not just safe but righteous by exiling those people whose disease defines them as unclean. An unclean man becomes socially dead to the community, and must be separated from everyone else, because his touch—like the touch of a corpse—will contaminate the pure.

Every culture has unclean people. They often have what are called "totalizing diseases" that remove them—physically and spiritually—from the community and make them almost non-people. In our time, for example, you might *have* a cold, but you *are* a schizophrenic; you lose your human and spiritual identity and become defined by that illness. And your presence in the workplace or the family or the church disorders everything.

Jesus steps right into this mess. "If you choose," says the leper, "you can cleanse me."

"I do choose," Jesus says, and touches the man.

This is a shocking statement about how God does things. Jesus doesn't just verbally proclaim the man clean—he sanctifies the man by taking on his contagion, physically *touching* him. Jesus' willingness to become unclean himself totally shifts the boundaries of order.

When Jesus enters into relationship with outcasts and shares in their social death, he starts a process of resurrection. The unclean become full, living people, born again. They are reincorporated—that is, re-bodied—into the community. And the community is healed into wholeness from separation, made new.

From the very moment of Jesus' incarnation, God has been doing exactly this: restoring creation to order by entering a human body; staying with us in the darkest, sickest places; taking on social and finally physical death, so that we can all become one and rise from the dead.

We're so used to thinking of the Bible as "religious" that Jesus' almost complete disdain for the business, as revealed in the Gospel stories, is disturbing. *Don't idolize religion,* Jesus reminds his disciples, impatiently.

Of course, all of us long for religion. In Jesus' time, every part of life—hygiene, food, sex, money, agriculture, economics, child rearing, health, ethics, marriage, death, and temple practice—was governed by a catalog of religious laws that attempted to shape human life to please the Divine. And although it's easy, at the distance of centuries, to mock a religion that specified exactly which fabrics were acceptable to God, we still share our forebears' desire to codify our lives in order to manage God.

Religion is a set of ideas *about* God, purified and abstracted from ongoing relationship *with* God. And from religion springs sin: the attempt to separate ourselves from others, the failure to see everyone as an inseparable part of God's body. The feverish wish to practice correct religion with the right kind of people. The inability to comprehend that other human beings, not like me, are human beings. And that they hold, precisely because they are *not* like me, the key to my salvation.

In the story of the Canaanite woman, Jesus has just finished talking with his disciples about religious practices, giving a wise and deep reading of the law that rejects the purity codes in favor of lived integrity. It's not how you wash your hands that pleases God, he's taught them. If you want to know God, the point is what's in your heart, not following a technical set of rules.

Of course, Jesus isn't making this stuff up out of nowhere, as too many Christians would still like to believe. Jesus is being fundamentally Jewish, echoing Moses, for example, with his emphasis on experienced grace over law. He's quoting David and the psalmists, who constantly remind their people that God wants a changed heart, not ritual sacrifice—or, as one psalm says, with bite: "a shattered heart I welcome."

So he's just preached a beautiful sermon about God's presence in our relationships with others. Jesus says that the nature of these human relationships—not obedience to ritual law—is what determines our relationship to God. You can't murder other people, slander them or steal from them, and claim to be right with God.

And then this woman comes up. This woman is definitely a religious outsider to Jesus and his followers. Scripture was full of stories about the evil Canaanites, who occupied the promised land, and their disgusting religious practices—worshipping idols, sacrificing children, and marrying people of other faiths, among other abominations. This woman belongs to the most despicable religion, from a Jewish point of view. And, to top it off, she's a persistent whiner and wants Jesus to heal her daughter, something she is totally unqualified to ask for.

So Jesus, righteously, tells her to shut up and go away. "I was sent only to the lost sheep of the house of Israel," he says. In essence, "You aren't my people." In fact, he means, you aren't really human. You are a bitch, a dog, an animal.

story from this point on is often presented as a healing story. And it is, but it's one of the edgiest and most frightening in the Gospels, because it's about the healing of Jesus. Jesus, through God's grace, is healed of his racism by the Canaanite woman. Jesus is healed of his fully human desire to make boundaries instead of experiencing love. Jesus is healed, by an abominable outsider, of the sin of religion, which seeks to separate the indivisible parts of God's creation.

And Jesus becomes the cure for religion.

In the falling away of religion, if we are to believe the stories, all our anxious human rule-making is replaced with, finally, mercy. The parables of the prodigal son, the generous landowner, and the dishonest steward all reveal the teaching thrust of Jesus' life on earth. God is merciful without reason, he tells us repeatedly, so *have mercy.*

Jesus ignores his good and upright hosts, and announces that a sinful woman is forgiven everything, because she loved so much. He tells his bemused followers that the laborer who works for an hour should get as much pay as the one who works all day; that one lost sheep is more important than the ninety-nine safe ones. He points out that even the birds are fed. Jesus proclaims, as Billie Holiday would later sing with the same unfair sweetness, "Them that's got shall get, them that's not shall lose."

These words remain challenging, because it's so tempting to believe there are good people, who should be rewarded, and bad people, who deserve their problems, and that God will sort things out fairly according to our own ideas about justice.

And yet Jesus' very life tells us something different.

Despised, rejected, rebuked, scorned; betrayed, abandoned, captured, judged; sentenced, scourged, and killed: this is not a story of justice. God is not just to Jesus.

And yet, in Luke's Gospel, after he's forgiven the friends who betrayed him and the soldiers who bound and beat him, Jesus, the tortured criminal, turns to the tortured criminal hanging next to him and promises paradise. Mercy hangs on the cross.

Then, the story says, Jesus gives over the Spirit, and breathes his last.

It is not the end.

Everything Jesus has revealed, through stories and parables, bossy directives and patient touch, remains available to his disciples. He's shown that we have the power not just to feed and heal, forgive and cleanse, but to do these things in new ways that reflect God's nature and give us life.

It doesn't take a special kind of person—the selfish and obtuse are welcome, too. It doesn't take a lot of equipment, or training—little kids can lead. Jesus is still with us, which means we can say *yes* to God's call, without knowing what the outcome will be. We can jump right in, instead of waiting for a committee to authorize our work. We can come and see what God is doing, all over the place, instead of worrying that we're not good enough. We can get over our fear of strangers, free ourselves from superstition, and find sweet streams of mercy in the middle of the world's driest places. We're not alone.

feeding

Once, at the food pantry, an old woman started speaking in tongues. Sometimes people who didn't understand each other's languages—a Tagalog speaker and a Nicaraguan, for example—would have actual conversations together over lunch. Once I saw a man pick up a big bunch of collard greens and hold it high, like a ceremonial staff, and wave it in blessing. Often I saw people poke the tomatoes suspiciously, casting off the rotten ones, sneaking extra vegetables into their friends' bags, and then the thieves would kiss the honest workers. Sometimes I ate standing up, or sitting on the curb, or leaning on the baptismal font, and the holy water and candy wrappers and overflowing compost bin all swirled together around the edges of my vision, along with the chatter of hundreds waiting in line, as I held my plate of spaghetti.

The concrete experience of the food pantry, like the Gospel, is stuffed with stories like this: because anywhere there's food, spirit and matter intersect. And the power to feed—and particularly to share food with

21

people outside your tribe—always has the potential to transform lives.

✠

The food pantry at St. Gregory's church began in 2000, and has been open virtually every Friday since then, offering free groceries to anyone who shows up. It's run entirely by volunteers: poor people who came to get fed and stayed to feed others. It's funded entirely by donations, not foundations or churches. We buy food for just pennies a pound from the nonprofit San Francisco Food Bank, which delivers truckloads of fresh produce and dry goods from its warehouse every week.

Somehow, over the years, the pantry has managed to exist in a strange zone both intensely real and kind of otherworldly. One afternoon, I found a worn-out man kneeling in the back of the church by an icon of Sophia, the Wisdom of God. I offered to anoint him with some holy oil, fragrant with rosemary, from a little container we keep in our shrine. "Ahh," he said, receiving it. "That feels *so* good." A few minutes later a little kid came over, by the same icon, and handed me a toy fire engine. "Want to play trucks?" he asked.

The food pantry has kept getting bigger and stronger and more beautiful, despite our best efforts at controlling it rationally. We despaired of feeding as many as two hundred people a week, then we fed four hundred, then five hundred, then, as the economy collapsed, eight hundred. I was hopeless at conventional fundraising: I couldn't get

22

it together to ask for grants from churches or foundations or the government. But individual donations, in tens and twenties and thousands, kept coming in. We used the money to help start eighteen other pantries, in churches and community centers, housing projects and schools. We gave away seed grants and advice to people like the short, tough Mexican pastor who came one afternoon and stood speechless in the middle of the chaotic food distribution for forty minutes, then said, "This looks more like Jesus than anything."

I looked around to see what he meant. It looked like a mess to me. An old lady in a straw hat was pushing her grocery cart up to us. It was jumbled full of potatoes and onions. "Hi there!" she crowed, giving me a big kiss that smeared lipstick on my chin. "Goodness and mercy gonna follow us," she pronounced, apropos of nothing at all. "God is good, *all* the time."

Michael snorted when he heard people talk like that. Our operations guy, and a food pantry board member, Michael was a streetwise Irish ex-con with a bunch of missing teeth, rough tattoos, and a genius for systems. He'd whipped our crew of fifty mismatched volunteers into what he boasted was "a well-oiled machine." Some-times, I thought, the oil spattered everywhere and the gears seemed held together with baling wire. But Michael, with his constant barking supervision and exhorta-tions, made it possible for us to become the biggest and most efficient pantry in the city, as well as a place the volunteers described, matter-of-factly, as their "church" or "family."

We didn't have a lot of rules. You could *be* a drunk or a junkie, but you couldn't volunteer if you were high. You couldn't steal food, call people names, or get in fights.

Otherwise anyone was welcome to jump in and start working. We were making a bet that what Jesus suggested was true: when you begin to expand your ideas of who the right people are, when you break down boundaries to share food with strangers, God shows up.

The pantry wasn't big on meetings. We certainly never had meetings about "diversity." Yet the volunteers who claimed this as their family were wildly diverse: conservative evangelicals, Russian and Greek Orthodox believers, Catholics, Hindus, atheists, Jews, Buddhists, agnostics, even an Episcopalian or two. There were gay Chinese American guys, black church ladies, Filipino seniors, Latina moms, European punks, Japanese students; people who lived on the streets and people who lived in nice houses; mentally ill men, young women with drug problems, disabled people, little kids, even a couple of beautiful babies. It was hard to imagine who *wouldn't* fit in here—kind of like the kingdom of heaven.

"Every now and again we get someone who thinks, 'Oh a bunch of Christians, this will be easy,'" Michael told me, explaining how he brought new volunteers into the fold, when he suspected they were going to try a scam on us. "I give them about an hour to think they have it figured out, then jam them and tell them the score and a warning. At that point they leave or knuckle down."

He lit a cigarette. "It's not about individuals, more like one body or many working as one team where each individual makes it all work." Michael smiled at me, embarrassed. "God, this sounds like all that motivational speaker type shit," he said.

It sounded, actually, like Jesus. When evening falls, goes the story, the disciples approach him and say, "This is a lonely place, and time has slipped by; so send the people away to the villages to buy themselves some food." Jesus replies, "There's no need for them to go: give them something to eat yourselves."

Winding up at the shore of a lake without enough ritually pure food of their own would have made believers anxious. And eating in the company of people of unknown moral and religious character would have made everyone even more unsettled.

But Jesus consistently chose unconventional table fellowship as the sign of God's kingdom. And so faced with a crowd of five thousand, he drives home the message he's been preaching—about the spiritual unimportance of religious and social barriers—by inviting everyone to share a meal on the spot. The point is not food. It is hands-on learning. Do this, Jesus says, and you'll taste what life in the kingdom of God is like.

The kingdom of heaven is not privatized. It is not about commerce, about buying what you need for yourself. It is not passive: Jesus doesn't ask his disciples to wait for a miracle, but commands them, with a brusque authority worthy of Michael's, "*You* give the people something to

25

Because life in the kingdom means there's more than enough for everyone.

Jesus enjoins his disciples to participate in God's work. Then he takes the bread and gives thanks to God, to show them that the bread doesn't belong to them. Like everything we have, he says, bread comes from God, and your job is just to break it up and give it away. Give it to the wrong people, to the ones who haven't washed their hands correctly, to the latecomers and the women, to anyone who's hungry.

Jesus shows the disciples and the crowd that there is always enough to go around: God's economy is one of abundance, not scarcity. By giving away the things God has given us, by giving as profligately and unconditionally as God does, we receive everything we need.

We'll stay hungry if we eat alone. We'll be lonely if we think we can only share fellowship with the right people. We'll starve if we believe that a community is a supernatural kind of miracle, or a product we can buy—not something we create by offering ourselves recklessly to others. We'll never feel truly fed if we're constantly competing to get our share. If we believe that love is scarce, and are afraid to give it away.

But the good news, the promise of Jesus, is different.

Michael, who'd be horrified to be described as a Christian, was articulating, in his rough-edged practice at the food pantry, something very close to what Jesus showed.

26

We'd begin unloading our deliveries from the local food bank early in the morning, unpacking as much as nine tons of food from pallets and setting it up on tables in the church rotunda, farmers' market style. While the volunteers worked, tossing loaves of bread and heads of cabbage around like stevedores, Paul and I cooked "family meal"; we all sat down to eat lunch together around eleven. Then the volunteers got their own groceries, and at 12:30 we opened the door to a line of hungry families that stretched around the block. The rest of the afternoon would be chaotic, with crowds pouring through the church and staggering out with bags of food. Michael had organized the volunteers for a prodigious array of tasks: multilingual line management, door management, bathroom management; box breakdown, yard cleanup, street cleanup, kitchen cleanup; rice table, potato table, fruit table, and the unruly bread table, where occasionally a pair of grandmothers would come nearly to blows over some hamburger rolls. We had enough volunteers, but there was always something else to do.

It wasn't an efficient church ministry or food service business, and it wasn't magic. It was, as a new volunteer told me once in astonishment, a miracle—a handmade one. "You see the food we give away, piles of it, and then we have lunch, and suddenly you don't see it as raw stuff anymore, but a fabulous feast," Chris said. He'd been unloading cabbages and potatoes all morning, and had brought some extra scallions into the kitchen where Paul and I were preparing family meal. "Oh, man, mashed potatoes. I *love* mashed potatoes." Paul smiled, whipping more butter into the bowl. "It's like a miracle, to see how the food is cooked and eaten and shared," Chris blurted out. "And how we're all fed."

Michael and the volunteers and I were learning how to access something that could satisfy our most profound hungers. The sharing of food—and the sharing of work—was turning isolated individuals into a community, however unlikely or tenuous.

There are all kinds of communities, both accidental and chosen. There are the ones, like biological families or neighborhoods, that we're enmeshed in for decades, and temporary ones—like the group that's stuck in the elevator together when an earthquake hits. I was starting to recognize that the pantry was a very particular kind of community: it was, precisely, a church.

I couldn't really understand church community through applying metaphors of family or friendship. Within any church, of course, there *are* families, as well as special friendships, deep emotional relationships, people who share similar backgrounds or are in love with each other.

But I'd seen, at St. Gregory's, how a family dynamic could bring out all kinds of complicated psychological issues in the community. If the priest was supposed to be the dad or the mom, then who was the good kid, the bad kid, the crazy aunt? If the church was supposed to be our home, then everyone got stuck bickering with others like siblings, instead of being able to bicker like adults.

And I'd seen, sometimes to my chagrin, how church wasn't a friendship network. I hadn't picked the people at St. Gregory's, and they hadn't picked me. And even though we might like to think we had so much in common, we actually weren't bound together by having the same taste in art or the same political views or the same cultural interests. We were bound together by Christ's peace, which, notably, passes human understanding.

When I first started coming to church, I was shy and snobbish and terrified of the "fellowship" at coffee hour. I'd always loathed forced socializing, and I didn't want to make friends with people I didn't know. It wasn't until these strangers began working with me—teaching me how to sing, or asking me to help with the dishes—that I got glimpses of what a church community could mean.

It was the shared work of worship and service that made St. Gregory's a real community for me. Which is exactly what we were all discovering at the pantry. As we cooked and swept the floors, we accompanied each other through struggle, sickness, sadness, joy, death, celebration, and change. I began to see that any church community is a body—a living body that needs delicate and honest attention to thrive. It required caring for people who weren't my family or friends, people I might not especially like. It required throwing away romantic, idealized notions of how special and unique we were. It forced us to accept grace and comfort from strangers, and to keep opening ourselves to new people.

"It's an ashram here, honey," explained Nirmala. A petite Chilean woman who'd been saved from crippling depression by a Hindu guru, she was Michael's lieutenant, in charge of the pantry's indoor operations. Nirmala patted me briskly, pushing me out of her way as she set out coffee for the volunteers.

"This isn't just a food place," she said. "It's a spiritual place. The pantry is spiritual nourishment—there's a lot of karma you can work out with people here. We're all so different, but we elevate ourselves a bit here, spiritually, by being with each other."

Nirmala was less gruff than Michael, but far less sentimental. She lived austerely alone in a single-room hotel, free from the "bad choices"—drugs, a crazy boyfriend, the drama of the streets—that had briefly ensnared her before the ashram. "Oh please, honey, I don't have time for any of that," she'd announced once, when I asked if she missed having a lover. "I do my work here, I do my cleaning, I pray. That's it. No attachments. I'm like air."

But Nirmala had a soft spot for kids. She occasionally brought in Johnny, a mentally ill teenager she'd befriended when he was a small boy, and gave him lunch; she clucked over the young, overly made-up girls from Kazakhstan, undocumented immigrants so far from home. And when we were asked to host students from Downtown High School, Nirmala was the first to speak up for them.

Downtown was known as the city's "last chance" high school, for kids too troubled or difficult to make it anywhere else in the system; most of the students had probation officers, and very few of them had stable homes. There had been a lot of anxious neighborhood meetings when Downtown moved into the old school a few blocks away. On a bus or on the street, adults tended to shrink from Downtown kids. They wore puffy parkas and baggy pants, do-rags and tattoos, unlaced shoes, attitude. They traveled in packs and didn't step aside; they shouted out angry curses at each other, or slouched around sullen and silent.

But some of the kids had a teacher, the unbelievably named Miss Grace. A slender white woman with prematurely gray hair and steely patience, Miss Grace had called me one afternoon and asked if she could bring "a few of my cherubs" to volunteer at the food pantry.

"Great," said Michael, when I told him. He looked totally exasperated, and glanced around the room at a group of volunteers struggling with a unwieldy tower of cereal boxes. "Oh, great, now we'll add some juvenile delinquents to the mix," Michael grumbled. "On top of the thieves and the drunks and all those retarded guys, I mean, I know they can't help it, but Jesus, I have to keep an eye on them every second."

"It'll be good for the kids," I said.

Michael sighed. "I know," he said.

About twenty-five teenagers showed up, dubious about the whole endeavor. "Hi, honey," Nirmala sang out to a stony-faced girl. Miss Grace and Nirmala shook hands warmly. "Antoine, take off your headphones," said Miss Grace. "Shaundra. *Shaundra!* Put your backpack down *now.*"

"Over there," Nirmala pointed, and the high school kids, some still ostentatiously unimpressed, started unpacking food, breaking down boxes, hauling pallets. By noon it

31

was time for lunch—fried chicken, macaroni and cheese, and chocolate cake—and the kids watched, surprised, as we set up long tables and invited them to sit down with us to eat. "Do you got any ranch dressing?" one girl asked Paul, more or less politely, and he went into the kitchen to make some. "He *made* this!" I heard the girl whisper to her friend when he came out with a bowl. She poured it over her chicken. "It's, like, homemade." Miss Grace would later report to me that the kids were "blown away" by the tablecloths at lunch. "Nobody ever put a tablecloth on for us before," one boy said.

The next visit was a little easier. This time the kids came in the afternoon when the pantry was open, and put on aprons to serve, and something happened as they began to hand out food. Over and over, people took the bag of potatoes or the loaves of bread and smiled at the kids. "Thank you," they said to the boy with the scars on his face, the girl with the gang tattoo, the sullen kid with his hood pulled up. "Thank you, thank you."

A couple of food pantry volunteers fell deep into conversation with the teenagers. "Man, I know what it's like," said Walter. "White people were always afraid of me when I was that age." Elizabeth watched the kids trying to make themselves understood to elderly Chinese and Russian women. "These people could be their grandparents," she said. "But the kids never talk to them." I brought the students snacks as the afternoon went on: we served a hundred visitors, two hundred, three hundred; we ran out of bread, and the teenagers started passing out reserve bags of apples. "Thank you," adults kept saying to the teenagers. "Thank you."

A tall Latino boy with a gold tooth was piling up tall, symmetrical pyramids of granola bars when I stopped by his table. He'd been working for hours, and his area was meticulously neat. "Nice job," I said. He looked at me shyly. "It feels really good to give food away," he said.

That was the consensus: giving food away changed everything. Mona, a young Latina mother of four, started to cry when she told me about her first week as a volunteer. "When I was out of work," she said, "my sister brought me here, and they gave me a huge box of food, and I was so thankful I could feed my kids." She dabbed at her eyes with the corner of her new food pantry T-shirt. I'd had them made for the volunteers; the logo was a fist clutching an apple, in a kind of Socialist-realist style, with our slogan: "Peace on Earth and Food for All."

Mona had asked Nirmala if she could help. After a few weeks of volunteering, she brought in her mother to meet everyone. "When I was a teenager," she told me, "I ran away from home. I put my mom through so much. Then I decided I wanted to make people proud." Now she flirted with the old men, carried the grandmothers' bags up the church steps, and fussed over every child, slipping them all cookies or pieces of fruit. "I came here and was welcomed equally as a person who got food and a person who gives," she said. "So when I see other mothers with kids in line, I feel, wow, I've been there, and I'm just so grateful to be giving."

Giving was the basis for authority at the pantry: people became leaders because they worked hard and took care of others. As far as I knew, Michael had never in his life quoted Jesus—*the greatest among you must be servant of all*—but an ethic of service permeated the pantry he ran. Being the operations director, an entirely unpaid position, simply meant that Michael was the first to come and the last to leave, and that he took phone calls all week from troubled or complaining volunteers who wanted his counsel. Paul, the church's rector, got down on his knees to scrape pigeon droppings off the back steps; Nirmala, the second-in-command, jumped in to scrub the grease-covered stove. I tried to work as hard as they did, but could barely manage to walk through the church with a mop in my hand before someone grabbed it. "Sara," the volunteer would scold. "Let me do that for you." Bruce, a canny ex-Navy guy, shook his head watching us. "Everywhere else I've ever been, people try to avoid work," he said. "But here, it's like people are running *toward* the work."

Glen was one of them. A skinny, hyper white guy with long gray hair and a torn sleeveless T-shirt, he rushed through the pantry picking up tasks, sweaty with emotion. "I *love* this place, Sara," he'd say, with great intensity. "You know, this place has saved my life. I woulda jumped out a window if I didn't have it."

Glen went to a court-mandated anger management class, because he'd been in so many fights; his social worker, he said, couldn't believe he worked all day on Fridays without getting in trouble. But every week he walked for forty minutes to get to the pantry, then ran around unloading and cleaning, fixing the dishwasher on his knees, taking apart broken pipes, piling up boxes in the backyard.

He draped his arm around me. "I come here and I get to give everybody something," he said, sounding kind of stunned, but happy. "I don't have to like them. It doesn't matter if they're assholes; it doesn't matter what they say to me: I'm never angry here. I don't even want to fight. It's weird, I'm like a different person. I look forward to Fridays all week. It's the place I can just be with everyone, no matter who they are."

And then there were the Fridays I didn't look forward to at all. I'd show up already impatient, dreading conversations with one more crazy person. I'd snap at Paul and be rude to Michael; I'd cook morosely, not even bothering to make the lunch nice. I felt hateful sometimes, watching people trying to scam each other; I felt disappointed when, for the third week in a row, Big Jim would show up drunk and obnoxious and we'd have to send him home. I got sick of pantry visitors peeing in the bushes, throwing their trash on the church steps, breaking the branches off the flowering trees in our front yard. The worst was when volunteers would corner me to complain about each other or whisper accusations: this one's stealing food, that one passes extra to her friends, he takes too much bread. It's not fair, it's not fair, it's not fair.

35

It *wasn't* fair. I tried to remember what Jesus preached constantly: *mercy*. It sounded like an abstract theological principle, but I clung to it to keep me afloat in what was otherwise an inexplicable sea of human sin. *Mercy*. It was all that could help me give up my self-pity and judgment. All that could help us turn the food pantry—whose volunteers and customers were, after all, no nicer or better than anyone else—into a beloved community, despite our selfishness and backbiting.

On one particularly exasperating afternoon, I went to talk to a fourth-grade class from the private school right around the corner. The kids had come the week before to volunteer at the pantry, and their teacher had asked me to discuss the experience with them. "They have a lot of questions," she said, somewhat ominously.

They certainly did. I sat wearily on the classroom rug, surrounded by bright-eyed children who peppered me with questions about fairness—the same questions that were tormenting me and the adult volunteers. How do you know the people who come to get food really need it? How come some people have cars and cell phones but they still get free food? Do people take advantage of you? Why do some people act crazy or yell while they're waiting for food? What do you do to keep people from cheating?

How could I explain it? I thought, one more time, about the completely unworldly sentiments expressed in the words inscribed on St. Gregory's altar: "Did not the Lord dine with publicans and harlots? Therefore, make no distinction between worthy and unworthy: all must be equal in your eyes to love and to serve."

We had set up our food pantry right around that altar, but the words were going to be hard for fourth graders, with their acute sense of justice. They were hard for adults who were habitually generous, and quick to be compassionate with the "deserving" poor, but impatient with the cheating, hustling, dishonest poor. And, I had to admit, they were hard for me on days when I felt exhausted and fed up with giving food away to people who were ungrateful, unfriendly, uncooperative, and bent on grabbing more than their share.

Sometimes all you can do is take what Jesus gives you, and swallow that bread.

So I talked with the kids about the idea of "taking advantage," explaining that it was impossible to be taken advantage of as long as you were giving something away without conditions. "If it's a trade, then it's fair or unfair," I said. "But if I'm going to give it to you anyway, no matter what you do, then you can't take advantage of me."

"How many of you have ever taken the best piece for yourself, or stolen something?" I asked, raising my own hand.

Slowly, every hand went up. "How many of you have ever been generous and given something away?" Every hand went up.

"Yeah," I said. "You know, poor people cheat and steal and are really annoying. Just like rich people. Just like you. And poor people are generous and kind and help strangers. Just like rich people. Just like you."

I was trying not to sound like a proselytizing Christian nut, but I had to add one more thing. "In my church,"

I said, "we say that judgment belongs to God, not to humans. So that makes things a lot easier for us. We don't have to decide who deserves food."

The teacher cleared her throat and asked for final comments.

"I think the pantry's like a special zone," said a girl with braids and braces. "Where everyone gets the same."

"Like," said another, "if George Bush or a homeless guy came to St. Gregory's, they could both get stuff."

"I think," said another boy, thoughtfully, "it's cool how people can't take advantage of you. That sort of means the pantry is invincible."

We had everything we needed because we gave everything away: we were invincible because we offered power and authority, just like food, to everyone. It was one of those Jesus-freak paradoxes that could sound, on the face of it, ludicrous. *Whoever loses his life will save it; whoever is last will be first.*

And yet as I traveled around talking with other churches who ran food programs, a great deal of what I saw struck me as modeled on different values: those of what Jesus, scathingly, called "the world." Screening, testing, rationing, churches set up food programs that operated like the Department of Motor Vehicles or a welfare office. They established "intake procedures" and called the people they served "clients." They never had enough volunteers, because they only asked church members to volunteer. And the people who did volunteer tended to burn out—partly, I suspected, because they got so tired of having to constantly enforce indefensible rules and be bad cops.

A big part of the problem, paradoxically, was that people wanted to be good. Liberals, particularly, wanted to be good, and wanted everyone else to be good, so they hammered on the verses from Matthew's Gospel where Jesus tells his followers to feed the hungry, clothe the naked, visit prisoners, and do unto the least of these. Liberals didn't necessarily believe these activities were, in themselves, joyful or fun or exciting. Instead, they twisted their fellow congregants' arms into working on outreach projects as if feeding the hungry were a symbolic action guaranteed to win points in heaven.

I came to hate the phrase "those less fortunate than ourselves." It usually led to guilt-laden social action programs, where Christians resentfully but dutifully offered poor people various kinds of "services" at arm's length. At one cathedral I visited, I saw ten clergymen eating lunch by themselves in a huge, light-filled hall, while below them two hundred poor women, children, and men crowded into a shabby cafeteria half the size for meals on plastic trays. The staff there told me that the regular noon Eucharist attracted fewer than a dozen worshippers; apparently, nobody had ever thought to invite the people breaking bread at the soup kitchen just fifty yards away, or to make the connection between the two events. The bread of heaven and daily bread were utterly different things.

At another Midwestern parish, I toured a beautiful, locked, empty sanctuary with its beautiful, locked empty parish hall. The church's food pantry was housed underground in the basement, where supplicants for once-monthly grocery bags waited for hours in a cramped hallway to have multiple documents checked. The elderly church volunteers complained that it was an effort for them to carry the food downstairs. They never considered using the parish hall or the sanctuary, though, to feed people. "It's so sad," said the woman who showed me around. "Nobody comes to church anymore."

The connection between worship and service played out in the different ways churches organized their work. A parish that clericalized worship, allowing only ordained people to make top-down decisions, was not likely to give full authority to volunteers at its food pantry. A congregation that was suspicious of newcomers, where old-timers held tightly to power, was probably also going to erect barriers to keep hungry people from running the food programs that served them. A church that doled out communion like a prize for good behavior would also tend to restrict the groceries it gave away, asking people to prove that they "deserved" the charity.

In one scenario, where worship was private, static, closed, and conservative, service to the world was seen as "worthy causes"—something that interrupted and inconvenienced real church life, rather than defining it. In another, "social action ministry" was something right-thinking believers did, and prayer was merely a ritual, an old-fashioned distraction from saving the world.

"Two thousand years of Christian history, that's why," was Paul's ironic answer whenever I'd ask why a church did something a particular way. Why do we say the Lord's Prayer standing? Why is the altar fenced off? Why isn't the food pantry in the sanctuary? Why, for that matter, do we have to print the bulletin on yellow paper? Two thousand years of Christian history, he'd joke, so shut up. Paul had a deep appreciation of the tradition, but he was also acutely aware of the ways religious groups, throughout time, justified their own prejudices and choices by idolizing tradition. And how, more often than not, that unexamined response encouraged people to be passive—to accept things as they were, instead of seeing themselves as actors, as followers of Jesus with a mandate to do his work.

Paul and I had begun consulting with other churches around the country interested in developing new approaches to worship and service. We visited rich, establishment congregations where the clergy wore perfectly ironed vestments, and small, casual churches with hippie pastors in sneakers. We led workshops on music and prayer, telling people they could make the liturgy themselves, as our congregation did. We told how our food pantry kept growing, and explained it was run by poor people, for poor people. We talked with church musicians and lay leaders and food pantry volunteers and priests, asking them all to consider *why* they made the choices they did, and what they thought their work was.

Sometimes we met resistance, but mostly we were treated to flattery. People insisted that St. Gregory's liturgy was so unique and beautiful, our food pantry was so special, that they couldn't possibly do anything like it themselves. It was as if they wanted to explain away the possibility of their own power. Of course, they'd say, you can experiment as much as you like out there in California; we could never get away with that in the South. Of course you must have a lot of creative folks in your congregation, not like our boring Midwestern grandmothers. Of course you have a wonderful bishop, a lot of money, a better class of poor people, some mysterious kind of permission that allows you to be so cool and daring.

I wanted to cry. "What more permission do they need?" I asked Paul, back in our hotel one evening. " 'Receive the Holy Spirit' isn't enough?"

But I remembered how often at my own food pantry I was afraid of doing things a new way. And how resentful I could be, how grudging, when the Spirit blew me somewhere I hadn't planned.

I thought about the time I'd headed over to San Francisco General Hospital after work for a diocesan meeting on "area ministry," with others doing food pantries, hospital chaplaincy, community organizing. It was all fine, but I was sick of everyone. I didn't have the energy to listen to interminable reports in church-speak from inarticulate clergy, or to the annoying church bureaucrat who tended to lecture us on process. I knew they were all well meaning, but I'd been at work since 7:30 in the morning, and I was really not looking forward to squirming in my chair like a fussy third grader through one more official presentation.

I drove down to the hospital with Paul, who, because he was a such a superior Christian, instead of a crabby, pathetic one like me, had baked a Texas sheet cake for the meeting, a sort of huge low-class chocolate brownie with thick icing. I didn't care. "I don't even care," I said to Paul. "I just hope this is over soon."

We got out of the car, carrying the cake and some plastic forks, and I was still grumbling, and then a woman standing at the bus stop in front of the hospital waved at us. "Hey, what's that?" she asked. She was a skinny woman with a big, toothy smile.

"It's a Texas sheet cake," said Paul, proudly.

I didn't mean to, but I blurted out, "You want some cake?"

"Yeah," the woman said. "Oh, yeah, that looks great. I haven't eaten all day."

Paul got a little plastic fork, and I cut off a piece and handed it to her, and she ate it and said, "Wow,

43

that's amazing; that is *so* good," and we all laughed, and I went into the meeting feeling undeservedly, irrationally, full of joy.

I wasn't living in hell anymore—the hell I'd made for myself out of self-righteousness, self-pity, and blame. I was, instead, at the feast prepared for everyone from the foundation of the world. And all it took was trusting my own authority to give away something delicious without waiting for the right moment, without claiming I was too overworked and putting it on my to-do list of good deeds.

I saw it happen in others when I traveled with Paul. Every time, we'd meet people who blew me away with their faithful willingness to jump in. Some were church professionals; some described themselves, humbly, as "just another soul in the pews"; and some had left church altogether. But all of them had felt Jesus breathing down their necks, tapping them on the shoulder, telling them not to wait, that they had the power to do things.

A Catholic woman wrote to me to say she ignored the anxiety of her priest ("Since Jesus loves the knuckleheads who are running things I must try to, also, but I don't have to agree with them") and opened the doors of the parish hall for a weekly free lunch. A Lutheran minister left her congregation of fifteen years in order to start, unsalaried, a center where anyone could drop by for rest, conversation, and food. "After all," she said, "I'm Italian. You have to give people something to eat." And an Orthodox priest involved with liturgical reform told me he was convinced that his faith depended on creating "not a church of laws, bishops, or customs so much, but a comm... Love rules. Very hard, but the only joy."

Joy. I saw it in people like Debbie Little Wym.. who'd founded a "street church" on Boston Commons that wound up inspiring a network of nearly a hundred outdoor churches. Debbie was a small, pale woman, with a great laugh and rimless glasses that made her look like a cross between a nun and a mad scientist. She told me that she began by just taking sandwiches to the park. "It was the oddest thing," she said. "I had an itch that wouldn't go away. I just had this crazy desire to get closer to people on the street, to see what Jesus meant."

Debbie had battled with herself about leaving a high-paying professional job to become a candidate for the priesthood; then she battled with the church about her calling to be a priest without a building. It took years. "Like many street folks," she said, wryly, "I guess I've never liked going indoors." A day after her ordination, she started her ministry without any more plan than packing a knapsack with peanut butter and jelly sandwiches.

As she told it, she bought two cups of coffee at a café, then wandered into the Boston Commons, looking, she said, for "someone on a bench who looked homeless." Debbie spotted a man and went over and sat down. She was full of doubt. "I had no idea what to say. I handed him one of the cups of coffee. He took it and he looked at me and said, 'So, how are *you* doing today?'"

Debbie laughed. "*Wham*," she said. "Five minutes in, and I guess I saw who was taking care of whom."

Debbie traveled all over now, helping start new outdoor churches, and there was hardly any kind of human misery she hadn't been very close to. Yet she was the least morose, most curious person I knew. I'd see her on the streets of Memphis and San Francisco, peering eagerly into the faces of people on the sidewalk, leaning over a heap of blankets and rags in a doorway, handing me a cup of yogurt with the same delighted smile she beamed at a drunk on the corner. That "crazy desire to get closer" was completely undiminished.

I looked at Debbie and thought I could never do what she did; other people looked at me and thought they could never do my work. It was true each of us had a particular style, particular weaknesses—but those weren't excuses for inaction. The truth was that anybody, at any moment, was capable of just taking one step closer to the Boyfriend's outstretched hand.

The hunger for connection wasn't something only Christians longed for. I'd thought, when I first started serving in church, how much it reminded me of working in restaurants. But I didn't realize that restaurant people might also be looking for a way to create, in their hot kitchens and crazy rushed services, an experience of communion.

Anthony Myint, like most of the line cooks I've ever known, displayed a very particular kind of masculinity.

He'd grown up in Virginia, the son of ethnic Chinese Burmese immigrants, and wore ironic glasses and a little goatee. Anthony didn't talk much, and he'd give uninflected emo shrugs if you asked him what he thought about something, but he was unquestionably in charge in a kitchen. His powerful arms were covered with burns and scars, he picked up hot pans without wincing, and he could taste with almost spectrographic precision.

San Francisco was full of young, hip, smart cooks like Anthony, but the failing economy was making it harder and harder for them to get anywhere professionally. The idea that a talented cook could raise a couple million dollars from investors to open a new concept restaurant was, as Anthony said flatly, "over." Nobody had the money to deal with real estate and building permits and picking an interior designer and creating a menu. Nobody believed, anymore, that even a place like San Francisco contained a limitless supply of financial sector professionals willing to drop a couple hundred dollars on dinner.

And Anthony disliked the whole restaurant culture anyway. He and his wife, Karen Leibowitz, lived in the Mission—my neighborhood—with its unpretentious mix of Latinos, slightly shabby hipsters, street people, and working-class families. They talked constantly about a way to avoid what he called "that stupid thing where your whole life is about the profit motive." He dreamed of launching a "charitable chain" of restaurants that gave away their profits. Not, he hastened to point out "to try and do something good," but as "a viable marketing strategy that's also socially conscious."

47

Karen, a deep thinker and natural organizer who'd finished her doctorate in English literature at Berkeley, had less interest in being a businessperson. But she believed Anthony could create a new business model by serving "food without attitude" and giving away profits to community groups. Karen didn't want to be taken for a bleeding heart, just because she was blond and soft-spoken, but she'd thought a lot about what she called "a way to give thanks for our comfortable lives," and how a restaurant could build community.

Their first venture was street food. Heading home one night after a shift, Anthony noticed that the taco truck on a neighborhood corner wasn't there; apparently its owners took Thursdays off. "I want to rent that truck," he thought. Soon hundreds of cool kids were lining up at the truck window for grilled flatbread and Anthony's friend's desserts, served at bargain prices on the sidewalk. And when they outgrew the taco truck, Anthony found a run-down Chinese joint, Lung Shan, and bargained to use its kitchen one night a week for the next incarnation of the project they called Mission Street Food. There'd be no reservations, and they'd set up a "community table" at the back of the little room for unaccompanied strangers. Anthony invited proposals from guest chefs, and promised to give the profits from each evening to a local charity. Karen waved away the idea that they were doing anything radical. "We make some money, and give some away—it's not complicated. Earnest but not deep, that's our niche."

But Mission Street Food had turned into the hot new thing. Anthony's buddies from the line, some geeky charcuterie stars, and a genius pastry chef known for his homemade salt-and-pepper ice cream were doing turns there. The local food blogs were raving. In a moment of show-offiness, I'd submitted my own proposal, hoping to raise money for the food pantry.

"I'm a former restaurant cook and war correspondent," I wrote. "I worked as a journalist for years, then ate a piece of bread and found God. I now feed 750+ a week in Potrero Hill at a church food pantry and cook a 4-course family meal for 45+ volunteers there with my sous (and the priest) Paul. I've lived in the Mission for 15 years, and raise chickens, apricots, figs, apples, lemons and plums in our backyard.

"I'd like to cook a neighborhood meal, with the crucial addition of swine." I paused, and sent an e-mail to Paul. He was away on a pilgrimage in Ethiopia, so I knew he wouldn't read it for a while. "Hey," I said, "we're gonna cook a benefit meal for the pantry, OK?"

Then I turned back to my proposal. In a final burst of foolish pride, I wrote, "I can deal with weird kitchens."

From the street, Lung Shan was an unremarkably crappy Chinese restaurant, with a long take-out menu taped to its door. Inside, metallic posters of horses, heroic soldiers, and landscapes lined the walls; the Formica-covered tables were set with plastic glasses, paper napkins, and chopsticks. But the working space was terrifying:

Anthony led me through a warren of tiny rooms, each containing pieces of the kitchen. One room, the size of a twin bed, held a rice cooker, a freezer, some gallon jars of MSG and garlic powder, and a hot plate. Another had a refrigerator and shelves of unmatched plastic rice bowls. A larger space had stainless steel sinks and some stacks of boxes. We slid around a corner and through a narrow doorway. "Here we are," said Anthony. I looked at the four-burner stove, the deep fryer, and a griddle with giant holes cut out for woks. The floor was covered with flattened, grease-stained cardboard; and some kind of burnt scum was floating on the surface of the fryer. A row of overturned buckets held piles of set-up ingredients: sliced onions, garlic, a battered bowl of mysterious meat nuggets. A Chinese cook in a stained blue shirt turned a lever, and the flame whooshed up like a blowtorch. He ladled some brown liquid into the wok from a large tin can and then swirled it around expertly. The room was about a hundred degrees.

"Oh," I said.

"You can put your mise here," said Anthony, gesturing at the mess.

In most restaurant kitchens, the mise-en-place is arrayed in neat stainless steel containers over a low refrigerator. In most restaurant kitchens, for that matter, there are long, clean counters to chop on, a place to plate food, and a steam table. In most restaurant kitchens, there's water.

"You can get water from the room where the sinks are," offered Anthony. "Or just keep some by the stove."

I nodded, and kept taking inventory. The oven could hold only a single half-size sheet pan. The salads would have to be plated on top of the freezer in one of the other rooms, along with desserts. The rice cooker worked, but apparently if you plugged it in at the same time as the electric griddle, you'd blow a fuse.

"Did I tell you that Lung Shan is going to keep doing takeout while you cook?" asked Anthony. "You'll get one wok, the stove, and the fryer, but their cook will be working next to you, so you won't be able to use the griddle or that side of the room."

No counter, then. And no prep space. "You'll have to do the prep somewhere else," Anthony said.

I didn't want to ask, but I said casually, "So are there pots? Trays? Tools? Tongs?"

Anthony looked at me expressionlessly. "We can look," he said. "You might want to bring your own." He led me out the back. "Um," he warned, "this basement is kind of ghetto." Down the stairs was a dingy cellar where Anthony kept some pots and pans, and where Lung Shan stored staples. In the dim light I could see a broken recliner, and a sofa that looked as if someone had died or given birth on it.

"Cool," I said, too brightly.

Paul, when he returned, was kind. "Anthony told me they've got a hundred people waiting in line before they open on Thursday nights," I moaned. "Shit, this is insane."

"It'll be fun," said Paul, who had never worked in a restaurant before.

"And we have to get all the food cooked at the church, then drive it over, and there's no oven," I said.

"Honey, it'll be fine," he said.

"Fear not, fear not, fear not," I grumbled. "Oh, by the way, that reminds me, did I tell you we're also going to do midnight mass? I talked to Karen, and she said it would be okay if you wanted to celebrate communion after dinner service was over."

"At the *restaurant?*" said Paul, sounding incredulous. Then, patiently, "Sure."

Anthony and Karen came to visit the food pantry, and stayed for hours. They decided to turn over another night's profits, from Anthony's own cooking, to us. "This is the kind of thing we want to be a part of," Karen said. "I can't believe how many people you feed." And she wrote, on their blog, "We're really excited about the upcoming Food Pantry benefit night."

I was sleepless. Over the next few weeks, I'd make and remake the menu in my mind, drawing up obsessive prep lists and schedules. We planned to feature food gathered or grown in the city: foraged wild radish and fennel from a park, lemons from backyards, local walnuts, herbs, and vegetables from neighbors' gardens. Paul and I were exhausted with planning by the time we wrote the final menu: pork braised in milk, a no-meat rice and beans to appease the vegetarians, spicy mustard greens, hibiscus-beet ice cream, and our wild weed tart prices were under $10, except for the item we printed at the bottom of the menu. "Bread & Wine: Free," it read. "Eat with Jesus at midnight. All welcome, no restrictions, nothing for sale."

Karen, who'd grown up secular until, in the fourth grade, she became "interested in God" and asked for a bat mitzvah, had been gracious. "Like every Jew in America," she pointed out, "I'm used to living in a world that assumes Christianity." She wasn't threatened by Jesus, nor worried that offering communion at the restaurant would be divisive. But Karen wanted me to understand that it was her upbringing as a Jew, though no longer a particularly religious one, that led her to believe in doing good. "Not to get into heaven," she said, "but for its own sake. It's not reward oriented, or a paying back—no offense—because Jesus died. I mean, we make heaven here."

Anthony didn't seem to have an opinion about communion; he didn't have a big opinion about religion of any kind. His only doubt was the rice and beans. "I'm no expert, but I really think there is a direct relationship between the percentage of bacon–ham hocks–smoked meat and deliciousness," he wrote. "You already have a vegetarian option, so I might be in favor of delicious-ness here."

At some point on the morning of the benefit, as I was wrestling a pork butt out of its brine and sealing up the five-gallon crock of preserved-lemon chowchow, I glanced at the clock. There were only thirteen more hours left on this shift.

The night itself passed in a blur. We turned the place over four times, serving around 250 meals. Paul, wearing a kerchief knotted over his head, manned the wok, burning the hair off his forearms as he literally dripped with sweat. Anthony made flatbreads, Karen worked the front of the house, and an assortment of waiters and food runners and kitchen helpers moved through the tiny rooms at warp speed. Deb Tullman, a young St. Gregory's member who worked at one of the city's most upscale restaurants, volunteered to wait tables. AnnaMarie Hoos, another church member who'd heroically chopped and diced for days of prep, was there to dine. Through it all, Lung Shan's skinny takeout cook kept turning out containers of fried rice and vegetables.

We celebrated Eucharist at midnight in the middle of the dining room, lit by strings of Christmas lights glinting off the metallic horse posters. My feet hurt more than they had in twenty years, and my shirt was slippery with grease. The waiters and dishwasher came out, curious, as I handed Paul a loaf of French bread.

He held it up, saying the ancient Hebrew prayer. "Blessed be God, ruler of the universe, who brings forth grain from the earth," he chanted.

"Now we share the bread with each other," Paul instructed. He was still wearing the kerchief, and his face was shining. "It's Jesus' table, so the bread is for everybody."

Karen looked exhausted, but she was standing nearby. The hipster waiter, Adam, was drinking Jamison's from a teacup. Anthony and his sous-chef, Emma, were at an uncleared table with a couple of friends. AnnaMarie and a few customers lingered. Deb, her posture still straight and her thick, curly hair pinned up, came close. I remembered how Deb had told me she didn't think communion was a good idea. "It's not gonna fly," she said. "At the end of a shift everyone just leaves as fast as they can, or maybe goes out to get drunk. But nobody wants to hang out in the restaurant." We passed the bread around, then a plastic glass of wine. The Boyfriend stood among us. I was a little embarrassed, and unbelievably happy. Paul nodded at me.

"Come, all who are hungry," I said, repeating the prophecy of Isaiah that we used for a post-communion prayer. "Come and eat, without money, without price. The Lord has made a promise to love you faithfully forever: you shall go out with joy, and be led forth with peace."

"Amen!" Paul said. "Amen," said Deb, a little shyly.

"And now we all hug and kiss each other," said Paul.

And we did. "Peace," I said to Karen, kissing her.

"Paz," the dishwasher said to me.

Adam hugged Paul awkwardly. "Peace," Paul said. "Is there any more of that whiskey?"

"Here," said Adam. "Have some of mine."

The hostess came over with a stack of bills. She was a tall girl, with elegant shoes. "I know Anthony and Karen are going to give you the profits from tonight," she said.

"But I want to give you my tips, too. Can you use it to get more food for your pantry?"

Deb came over, shaking her head. We sat down. Another of the waiters slipped me forty bucks. "That's it," I said. "That's communion."

"Wow, that was wild," Deb said. "Everyone was like, oh, ritual. Like we needed it but didn't know what it was. It's really different to end the night thinking, we made something together."

Karen joined us. "This customer wanted to talk to me about Mission Street Food tonight," she said. "He was visiting from Texas, and wanted to know how to start a restaurant like this where he lives. He said he imagined that they could do a similar thing in the church basement." She laughed. "And I thought, oh, hmm, I guess we invented church."

Mission Street Food was only one of the places in the neighborhood where people shared food. Around the corner from my house was a little playground called "Niños Unidos," built on an empty, weedy lot by a bunch of parents who fought the city for years to reclaim the space. As soon as the playground opened, it became full of kids climbing and running and screeching happily all day long, and every Sunday it hosted a free farm stand.

The stand was run by a guy called Tree—a shy, skinny, ponytailed old hippie with a scratchy voice—who thirty years ago had planted hundreds of fruit and nut trees on the streets of the barrio. If I was a Jesus freak, Tree was a tree freak: mad for sycamores, almonds, jacarandas, London planes, magnolias, apples, maples, flowering pears. He tended at least four community gardens, including a gigantic, verdant piece of paradise behind his rather crummy apartment, fenced with bamboo and dense with persimmons and poppies. The first time I met him was at a town meeting where he stood and introduced himself to the mayor: "My name is Tree, and I care about the trees." Earnestly, he added, "I care about the mature canopy."

"I just love trees," he told me once, "but I *really* love the idea that people can eat from trees. I don't object to ornamentals, but when I moved to the Mission I wanted to plant food." Now Jordanian ladies picked almonds from little sidewalk forests he planted back in the 1970s, and Mexican teenagers gathered figs from trees planted before they were born.

When Niños Unidos was built, Tree started a community garden there, and divided it into plots and showed other people how to join him in growing food. He built raised beds and staked some espaliered pear trees along a chain-link fence. Then he set up a little table to give away the extra produce from the garden—beans, herbs, apples, squash, kale—and dug up seedlings and gave them away, too, so other people could have plants.

He offered tips on composting, collecting food scraps from kitchens and hauling them away on his bicycle. He went to neighborhood after-school programs and began teaching the kids to weed and water and prune. He wrote a blog, interspersing advice about potato towers and drip irrigation with praise for "the beautiful miracle of gardening" and gratitude for "being connected to the love energy out there." He scavenged manure, borrowed wheelbarrows, and built another garden in a new nearby lot. And then other gardeners—people who didn't even know Tree—started bringing the surplus food from their home gardens to share at the farm stand.

Soon more neighbors showed up, bearing big bunches of roses and wildflowers, and giving away buckets of ripe tomatoes. The playground parents began swapping recipes: here's what to do with fava beans; hey, try these striped squash. A few urban beekeepers offered little jars of honey from hives they kept around the city. Tree, who also kept bees, found a new friend who'd studied classical languages and would read aloud to him from Virgil's *Georgics* as they worked the big extractor. "'Of air-born honey, gift of heaven, I now take up the tale,'" Tree quoted. "Oh, those Greeks and Romans really loved bees."

Then a bunch of garden nerds, church volunteers, and a high school teacher started organizing to glean fruit from the variety of trees that produce so profligately in San Francisco. Like the members of nearby Temple Emanu-El, who'd planted a garden on their cemetery in order to give the food away, they were inspired by the biblical command to leave excess food in the fields for "the poor and the stranger" to harvest. These modern gleaners printed up leaflets and knocked on doors, offering to pick backyard trees, leave whatever the owners wanted, and bring the rest to the free farm stand to give away. They scavenged in public parks as well, and from street trees.

Another group of urban gardeners offered to prune and care for the gleaned trees, and the circle widened. A slightly obsessed arborist who loved to talk about root stock designed a Google map for the group. It had pins showing every tree identified by the gleaners, and information on location, size, and approximate ripening time. By summer, there were a dozen people out harvesting throughout the city on the weekends, high school kids with ladders and buckets, guys in pickup trucks coming back with heaps of gleaned lemons and plums and oranges, offering it all to passersby at the makeshift tent in the middle of a garden in the barrio.

I walked over there one day after church with my daughter, Katie. Tree's blog the week before had been effusive with happiness. "If I could sum up my feelings right at the moment into one word," he wrote, under a photo of some lettuce, "it would be gratefulness. If a person doesn't get a chance to feel grateful, I would guess that would be a sad situation, because it is a great way of feeling high."

The garden was full of families, and fragrant with the scent of sweet peas. Tree gave us beets he'd grown, and then another woman gave us epazote that she pulled out of her bike basket, and then someone else gave us two gorgeous heads of radicchio. I promised a Guatemalan woman that I'd bring her plums from our tree as soon as they were ripe. "We have so many we don't know what to do with them," I said. "Good for eating, and for cooking."

Katie was amazed. "It's kind of like heaven," she said, watching everyone swapping food. We started to leave, and Tree ran after us shouting hoarsely, "Don't go! Wait!"

I turned around. "I have *pie!*" he said.

And he pulled out a gigantic blackberry pie he'd baked, with berries someone had picked from the side of the road up on a nearby hill. And we stood there at the side of the lake, with the crowd, and Jesus, and the homemade blackberry pie on a turned-over five-gallon plastic bucket, and Tree cutting up big pieces with a beat-up old knife and handing them to all of us under the mature canopy, saying, "Taste it; isn't that delicious? I made it for everyone. There's plenty."

God gives us everything we have, and whenever we are willing to receive that blessing and pass it on, we live in the kingdom of abundance. He gave the food to the disciples, who gave it to the crowds. And they all ate as much as they wanted.

✠

At the food pantry, it was our practice to bake something special for dessert when volunteers had birthdays. Some would announce the date proudly, and request their favorite—a rich tres leches or a German chocolate—to share at the lunch. Others, diffident, would only let it slip to a friend, who'd then come to find me in the kitchen and whisper the news.

"Honey," Nirmala said, "it's Michael's birthday today. You know he doesn't want a fuss; just do a little something." She poked Paul. "OK?" she said, and we went back out to the pantry to wrestle some bags of rice off the pallet.

When I came back to the kitchen, an hour and a half later, I was worn out. I'd met a Salvadoran woman named Gloria, whose best friend was dying; she'd come by to ask if she could pick up groceries for her. In the middle of our heartfelt conversation, I'd been interrupted by a fight between two volunteers. "Damn," I said to Paul. "Everybody had something going on today. Blah blah blah. Sorry to leave you alone with lunch."

Paul smiled. I looked over at the counter, where he was putting the finishing touches on a three-layer cake. It was pink and glistening, with little rosettes and scalloped edges. "Wow," I said. "That is really beautiful."

Paul stepped back, spatula in hand, to contemplate his buttercream icing. "Strawberry filling," he said, satisfied. "You know, when Michael was inside, in San Quentin, I bet he never thought anyone would ever make him a birthday cake again."

Michael shrugged off the birthday songs, though he blushed a bit when the cake came out and everyone cheered. He ate just a little piece, then went outside for a smoke. That day, he closed up the pantry, and I found him at the end of the afternoon leaning on the altar in the middle of the empty rotunda, going over our book to see how many pantry visitors had been through the line.

"You know, at the end of the day," he told me, "when you're counting up like this, and it's so quiet, you can't really believe 727 people have been here." He pulled on his jacket. "Yeah," Michael said, "you know I met a guy from the streets I hadn't seen for a long time, back when I was using. I told him my life story, and when I said I was running the food pantry in a church, he rolled his eyes."

"Was he surprised?" I asked.

"Hell yeah," said Michael. "He said, 'Why?' like I was crazy. I told him, because it matters that you get the chance to do something good with your life."

healing

I wanted to ask your help," said Julie. It was midnight on Easter, after a three-hour vigil service that began in the darkened church with a single candle and ended in a blaze of light, with dancing and joyous embraces around the altar. "Christ is risen from the dead, trampling down death by death," we'd sung, in half a dozen languages. "And on those in the tombs, bestowing life."

Now Julie and I were munching on ham biscuits, sitting in the sanctuary as the after-party swirled about us. Julie brushed away her long hair with a slender hand. She was a soft-spoken, fiercely intelligent doctor who'd come from Alabama to throw herself into medical care for the indigent. "I mean, we don't need to do it this minute, but I want to talk with you about healing."

I had no idea that the first conversation I'd fall into after celebrating the resurrection would be about healing. But over the next few months, Julie and I would collaborate with other doctors and caregivers to address their own fears, their sense of burnout and failure, and the needs of the people they cared for. And though not always explicitly "Christian," our discussions felt grounded in Easter: a Gospel of new life, based on what Jesus showed healing could mean.

⊞

Julie Tomford was thirty when she was made the chief of residents at San Francisco General Hospital, the legendary, underfunded county hospital that served the city's poor, sick, insane, and run over. The General was a frontline trauma center, taking care of women who were pushed out of windows, gangbangers stabbed or shot in the head, children caught in automatic-weapon crossfire, carpenters who sawed off their limbs, old men hit by buses, and the victims of every conceivable variety of motor vehicle disaster. The hospital had opened the first AIDS ward in the country; it set up its own wound clinic for junkies; its refugee clinic served palsied women in burkhas and tubercular Indians from Peru; and the emergency room stayed full, day and night, of cops, blood, kids with sore throats, and screamers. Lost souls thronged its psych units, though you had to be really, really crazy to actually get admitted to the General. One man who drank bleach to kill the bugs crawling inside his arms was treated, not unkindly, and sent back out to the streets. On quieter floors, nurses cared for people dying from cancer, diabetes, heart attacks, and liver failure.

Other hospitals might brag of their services with slogans like "Creating Excellence," but the ratty T-shirts worn by residents told a different story. "San Francisco General Hospital," they proclaimed. "As Real as It Gets."

Working at the General was not a job, its staff declared: it was a vocation. But heroics and piety aside, it was a vocation that frequently wore them out. "I feel like I'm hitting a wall," Julie said, when we started meeting after Easter to talk about healing. "I've always thought of myself as compassionate. I always wanted to treat addicts. Addiction is a huge boil on the backside of our society, and I don't want to be a part of the mass denial that allows it to be so underrecognized in medical contexts and so underfunded." She paused. Julie always spoke with great delicacy; every word seemed carefully chosen. "But I just can't feel hopeful with my patients anymore. I can't resist resenting and judging them for the lies they tell, and feeling like I'm making a personal sacrifice. I just don't *like* them, and I find myself thinking, wouldn't we both be better off if someone else were your doctor?"

It was the chronicity of her patients' problems, Julie said, that got to her. Their unwillingness to take responsibility for their health. You'd drain an abscessed wound, and run quarts of IV antibiotics through a junkie's arm, and three weeks later the same guy would be back, with a new infection from shooting up in exactly the same place. Then he'd shrink as you got ready to anesthetize and cut. "Doctor," he'd say, fearfully. "No, are you gonna put that needle in there? I'm scared of needles."

Julie looked at me. "You know when Jesus asks people, *Do you want to be healed?* I feel like so many people come to me, but they don't really want to be healed."

I knew what she meant. I was at the end of my own rope with Big Jim, who'd been part of our food pantry community for years. "He's killing himself," Michael said, disgusted, after Jim was diagnosed with cirrhosis. "He doesn't even see the irony that he'll die from booze, but he'll die sober, with his body shutting down in a hospital bed somewhere."

Jim savored hanging out at the food pantry: he talked soccer and politics and told long, earnest stories about his old life in the Haight Ashbury. He had a stutter and a terrible memory from his head injury, but he was an eager worker who'd help on the line and pick up trash outside the church for hours. One Christmas, Jim, who lived on disability, had brought in thirty little red envelopes with a dollar bill in each one, as gifts for the other volunteers. "Look," he said to me proudly, "there's one for everyone in our family."

But when Big Jim showed up drunk, he'd be spectacularly drunk: wetting his pants, knocking into things and falling down, howling incomprehensibly at people waiting in line for food. Michael tried to be patient. "Come back when you're sober," we'd say, one more time, as he threw himself on us in sodden embraces and pleaded to stay. "Oh, for Christ's sake, stop it, we love you too, but you know the rule." The weeks when Jim actually worked became rarer, and the nights when he phoned Michael in sloppy tears increased. The other volunteers were totally fed up with Jim: "Honey," said Nirmala, "he's very sick, I know, but he shouted at a lady on the line. We can't do this anymore."

Jim called Michael one night and promised he was ready to go to Alcoholics Anonymous. "I spent four hours on the phone, and was going to take him to a meeting," reported Michael, furious, "but then in the morning Jim called up saying he was too sick, and it turned out he'd bought a liter of vodka after we talked." Michael, who'd beaten his own heroin addiction fifteen years ago, had no patience for the chronic lies and excuses of addicts. "Jim doesn't want to get better."

"I think," I mused to Julie during one of our post-Easter meetings, "that Jim actually *does* kind of want to be healed. But it might not be what Michael or I think healing should look like—getting sober. It might just be feeling he's part of our community. That he's in relationship with us. We can't fix him or save him, but as long as we're connected, even if the relationship's messed up and makes us mad at him, Jim experiences some kind of healing."

Julie looked thoughtful. "It's like this Yemeni woman I see at my clinic," she said, "who just leaps up on the exam table, pulls off all her robes, uncovers her hair, and starts telling me her whole life story through the translator.

She's looking for healing, too. She always complains about muscle pain, terrible, terrible pain, and I can't really treat it. But she tells me she loves me, and I know she gets something from our visits. And oh, I do too. I can't cure her, but I *love* her."

She paused. "That's the hard thing about doctors, though," Julie said. "We really want to fix people."

"Sure, I'd like to fix people, too," said Anibal Mejía when I told him that Julie wanted to put together a group for burned-out healers. Anibal worked as a psychologist with homeless, mentally ill drug addicts, and he was also a priest in the Brazilian Candomblé tradition. "Wouldn't *that* be nice. But my job isn't to vanquish evil as much as to love."

Anibal had grown up in Arizona in a Unitarian household that carried vestiges of his parents' Catholicism, and endured a brief, uncomfortable time in a Methodist church where everyone else was white. As an unhappy young adult, living in Brazil, he discovered Candomblé de Ketu, a Yoruban religion related to Santería. He'd watched on the edges for a while, then passed through the rigorous, shimmeringly beautiful process of initiation into the mysteries of the *orishas,* or saints, with his "godmother," the priestess Iyá Marinete Martins de Souza.

A handsome, driven man with a wolfish smile, Anibal was an erudite writer. A scholar of religion as well as of psychology, Anibal maintained a sardonic running commentary on both systems.

Beneath all this worldliness, though, was faith. Anibal actually believed in God, as Scripture said, "with all his heart, and all his mind, and all his soul." He called Jesus "Friend," rather than "Boyfriend," but he was devoted. His decision to follow the orishas had allowed him to rediscover Jesus, as "a treasure I'd buried in a field."

He'd come to believe that the syncretism between Christianity and Yoruban religions wasn't casual at all. "It's actually a deep consideration of Christian teaching and a response to it," Anibal wrote to me. "I want to continue the contemplative practice of holding the two traditions up to my eyes and peering through them, as if through a glass darkly, until the Light/Love comes through and what is broken, or partial, reveals something true and whole."

In his job, Anibal worked under the same struggling city health system as Julie, treating many of the same people: damaged, chronically "difficult," and capable of driving even the most experienced doctor or therapist batty. "The saints tell us to hear our Friend's voice in all voices," he'd told me once, "but what do we do when the voices are saying, 'Fuck you, faggot!' or 'Could you give me a dollar? I need it for food,' when you know full well he's going to go get loaded on dope that's corroding his veins?"

I heard those voices too: in fact, one of my most out-of-control visitors to the food pantry, it turned out, was also a client of Anibal's. "I'm glad *you've* got him covered," I said once, after the man had left us screaming about the coming tribulation and the enemies he was going to kill. "I couldn't deal another minute." Anibal raised an eyebrow. "No problem," he said, dryly. "I told him everything was going to be fine, since Sister Sara was praying for him."

Just as I had found a connection between feeding and worship, Anibal believed his work as a healer and a priest was fundamentally the same. We'd sit and talk about it over lunch in the Mission, sharing our stories, reaching for an understanding of what it meant to have God living in bodies. "The mystery," I remember saying to him once, as we slurped some chicken soup, "the mystery doesn't have to be a secret, because it's there in plain sight all the time." Anibal sent me a note the next day. He'd been waiting for a client outside a single-room occupancy hotel, he told me, who was late for her appointment.

"I was leaning against a parking meter, bored," he wrote, "staring into the doorway of the Western Donut Shop, thinking what a dismal hole it was, how the donuts there were so bad that even I, veteran donut eater, wouldn't even think of eating these ones; appalled at the smell of greasy MSG 'Chinese' food; feeling sad watching drug deals and negotiations between whores and johns and pimps.

"Then another client I knew came up to me. He said, 'I like to look in there too. Because God's there.'

"I said, 'Yeah? How do you see that?'

"He said, 'The people. They sit for a while and eat. It gives them a little peace. I like to see it. It makes me know the world is good.'

70

"I couldn't say a word. Where I was seeing only grunge and poverty and a world falling apart, he saw something so different."

Anibal immediately understood Julie's dilemma: wanting to treat addicts, yet, increasingly, feeling hopeless. "I've struggled with much of the stuff she's talking about," he said. "I want to keep the conversation going about how we can do this and not get fried."

I decided to call Will Hocker, a chaplain at the General Hospital. I'd first met Will about eight years before, and our early relationship had a lot to do with healing—not just healing in general, but his own.

Will was a slender, sandy-haired man who hid impish humor under a deadpan, almost old-fashioned formality. A parishioner at St. Gregory's, he'd been a clinical social worker and psychotherapist, but had stopped working due to his own advancing AIDS and Hepatitis B. Soon after we met, he was hospitalized, and his lung collapsed. "I think this is bad," his husband told me when he called with the news. "In Chicago he almost died, but this time is really bad."

I remember Will, in a crumpled hospital gown, eyes bright in his sunken face, listening while a group of us from church sang around his bedside. He had one request. He'd been praying daily for another of our members, he said, a man who was dying of liver cancer, but now he was just too worn out to do it. Could somebody else take on the praying?

Prayer, new antiretrovirals, luck, obstinacy: whatever it was, Will stood up and came back to life. All that sickness burned something away, and he decided, late in his forties, to enter the process of postulancy to the priesthood. He fought his way through Greek and Hebrew and a whole new master's degree. He persevered through endless application forms and the most mind-numbing chapel classes at the Episcopal seminary, where faculty would instruct the postulants in the exact way to fold a surplice or compose their posture in the choir stall. He struggled with his husband, a high school science teacher, when Will, despite his nonexistent immune system, chose to do a semester of clinical pastoral education in an AIDS hospice in South Africa. "He might seem anxious sometimes," I wrote in my letter of recommendation to the bishop. "But Will is not afraid."

Will became an Episcopal priest. Now, in jeans and occasionally a clerical collar, Will roamed the halls of the General, listening and touching, praying and hanging out. He baptized stillborn babies, sat with weeping families, calmed traumatized staff, trained his army of volunteer chaplains, comforted the psychotic, and gave granola bars to anyone who looked hungry. "I'm spoiled," he told me once, explaining why he was relieved not to be the pastor of a fancy church. "Look at the work we get to do here in the hospital. We get to work with people who are unafraid of death of any sort, unafraid to cry, unafraid to get dirty, unafraid to speak the truth."

He grinned. "Plus," he said, "my people are really funny."

Will and Julie loved the work, but wanted to find a more sustainable way to do it. Julie, in particular, wanted to help her young residents learn to be healers, as well as doctors: people who could, as she said, "not get bogged down in the idea of effectiveness."

"I want to do good clinical treatment as much as anyone," she said. "But I need to give residents tools to measure the meaning rather than the effectiveness of their work, when medical outcomes point toward despair."

"Yeah," said Will. "I notice that a lot of doctors wind up really hating patients when they can't cure them. They get so angry when they can't fix things."

"I don't want to sound like a total Jesus freak—" I said.

"But you are," Will interrupted, smiling at me. Julie laughed.

"I know," I said. "But Jesus specifically heals people even when they aren't cured. He doesn't stop suffering, but promises to be with us in suffering."

There's a fine line between empowerment and bossiness. Jesus rampages through the Gospels wielding the imperative rather freely: *Get up! Don't be afraid! Follow me!* He commands: *You* get up and walk! *You* give the people something to eat! It's inspiring. When impatient and sometimes overbearing control queens like me do the same thing, it's just irritating.

Paul could be more subtle. "Not that I want to tell you what to do," he'd begin, in the kitchen, before telling me what to do. "More salt."

But Paul also understood how to wake up people steeped in the habits of church, who found it impossible to believe they really had the power Jesus breathed on them. His practice began with asking questions: *What do you want? What do you love doing?* In this, Paul was following the teachings of Gregory of Nyssa, who pointed out that we are most like God in our desire. Everybody desires something: even if you're shy or cynical or convinced that nothing will ever change, there's almost always something you want more of—just as God wants more of us.

And of course God, like human beings, enjoys it when everyone sits around eating and talking.

So I followed the example of Jesus, Gregory, and Paul: we cooked for the healers' workshop. About twenty-five people—doctors, nurses, social workers, psychologists, activists, chaplains—came to St. Gregory's one evening, as the last sun was glancing off the icons' halos. I stuck three chickens in the oven, pulled out the same tables we used for family meal at the food pantry, and set them with appetizers of bread and olives and wine.

Julie had invited people with years of experience caring for suffering, marginalized, and unwell patients, to talk about what they loved doing. There was a woman who ran what she called "Hepatitis C University," teaching junkies how to research and manage sophisticated treatments; a doctor who ran the methadone clinic at the General; a nurse who said his work in a neighborhood wracked by gang violence was making him "wonder about the existence of evil."

We got off to a shaky start. A peppy woman who billed herself as a "coach" was dispensing the kind of cheerful self-help advice that clogs the pages of magazines. If you were burning out and overwhelmed and couldn't stand your patients, "Try making some *me* time," she offered brightly. "Take the evening off, get a massage."

I could see Will Hocker, over at the side of the room, rolling his eyes. "Me time," he'd say later. "Like the problem with the public health system is providers just need to treat themselves to manicures."

Julie looked mortified. She thanked the woman politely and then stood.

"So," she said, "maybe we could talk about what we really want from this work. Why do you do it? What's the best part?"

I thought about what Julie and I had groped our way toward: the idea that healing was about creating meaning. What was our suffering, or the suffering of others, really for? Why were we going through this; what was the purpose? The search for meaning drove us all: doctors, nurses, chaplains, drug addicts, people with cancer. And we could only find it together, by telling the truth about our experiences, and listening to others.

In a way, we were hunting for the Gospel in our own stories. We were making midrash, not prettifying the narratives but exploring them for clues to our own lives.

"You know," Anibal had said to me once, "when you see lots of things that are broken, your feelings of cohesion and safety get threatened." He gestured to the rather sordid street scene outside the restaurant where we were having lunch. "But my religion allows me to see the broken stuff and stay in it."

The process resembled the way Jesus met the woman who was healed only after she "came in fear and trembling and fell down before him, and told him the whole truth." Sharing our real stories, unvarnished and unfinished, not only provided helpful tips or sympathetic laughs: it was the thing that allowed us to become whole.

The atmosphere in the church softened, as people began to tell the truth about their work. Anibal spoke about learning how to do case management. "The best thing for me was my teacher saying, 'Anibal, are you here to make people happy, or to help them make decisions about their health?'" He told about setting boundaries, about assessing the strengths of the most troubled people, about finding his own strength as a therapist through being honest about his weakness and need and fears.

He got in a few digs at doctors. "This one doc comes in and is mad because my client has liver disease, and says to him, 'You're a drunk; you're going to die.' Well, great, thanks, tell him something he doesn't know. 'Who else are you?' is the real question," said Anibal. "I see someone else in there, besides a drunk. Our job as healers is to help this person understand his own capacity to love and to heal."

76

Anibal stopped. He looked a little abashed, and I could see how difficult it was to get over the desire to be "professional," to act like an expert. But his honesty meant everything to those of us listening. "As a case manager and a priest, I've got to stop trying to save, convert, or help so much," Anibal said. "Just to awaken others and myself to life, inside us. If I can do that, it's good enough."

Will took a turn, talking about the days it felt impossible to get through the hallways of the hospital. "I mean, I'm late on my way to a meeting, and a patient's daughter grabs me, or I get waylaid in the elevator or get paged to the emergency room," he said. "I've got a grant proposal to write and e-mail to answer and a desk full of forms to fill out. I feel as if I'm constantly behind, constantly running to catch up."

Will gave a sweet little shrug. "So now I try to just lean *in* to the interruption," he said. "Slow down, pay attention. *This* is my real work, not anything else."

I listened to the methadone clinic director talk about what kept him going. "It sounds funny," he said, "but I think what happens is I just keep falling in love. With patients, with my staff, with my wife when I get home and tell her about the day. I feel this connection, and I want it to keep happening."

I thought about how what I wanted, and what these healers wanted, and what their sickest, most challenging patients wanted, were really not that different. In the short term, we all wanted fixes and ego gratification. We wanted to feel good about ourselves, to feel righteous or effective. We wanted the pain to stop, we wanted to get high, we wanted to correctly diagnose and cure the problem at hand.

But in the big sense, as Julie said, what we all wanted was meaning.

I sat there reflecting. I didn't really know how to find meaning—as distinct from the right answer—but I believed it was rooted in paying attention. Not just by noticing the cute-kitten moments, or the most ghastly ones, but by looking for things that were real between me and the people who came to me looking for healing; between me and the friends I worked with every day; between me and strangers. I thought about the mentally ill woman who came regularly to morning prayer. Just that morning she'd been standing in the church reading the Gospel aloud, with her hair wrapped up in a ripped sweatshirt, and I could see white streaks on her cheeks, the dried salt of old tears. I was antsy and preoccupied, worried about the thousand things I had to do, wishing I could finish the service and get to my desk. She turned and fixed her good eye on me. "Sara," she announced, "you need my prayers, so I'm praying for you."

I thought about Gloria, the Salvadoran woman who came to our pantry once in a while to pick up groceries for her dying friend and a teenage son. It sounded as if they lived in the nearby Potrero Hill projects, and I doubted Gloria had a job. But she always made a point of checking in with me. "Are you sure it's okay for me to take this food?" she'd demand. "I know there are a lot of poor people, and I don't want to take groceries if somebody else needs them more today."

I thought about finding a young black man on the church steps the week before, wearing a hoodie and holding his head in his hands. He scared me. But when I sat down beside him, it took only a minute for him to blurt out, "I had a fight with my mom this morning," and I saw he was just a frightened kid. I took him inside and gave him some breakfast, and while I was pouring the juice I was overcome with gratitude that my own daughter had made it through her adolescence feeling cared for by a series of roommates, neighbors, friends. Thank God, I thought, for grown-ups who spoke kindly to Katie on the mornings I yelled at her.

I thought about this very meeting: how I wished to be strong and powerful, and admired for my wonderful intellect, and always right. But how thin that was, finally. How much less interesting than what was here in right in front of us, as we ate our roast chicken and spilled out the messy truths of our stories. What I really needed was to be going forth into the world following the Boyfriend, with these people at my side, to see what else we could find.

That desire, that curiosity, had brought me into work as a healer when I started regularly attending St. Gregory's. The priest in charge of pastoral care, Lynn Baird, had developed a community-based network of lay caregivers who offered practical and spiritual support. In this model, pastoral care wasn't the property of the single traditional overworked parish priest who hears confessions, visits the sick, counsels troubled souls, and manages the health of an entire dependent congregation. Instead, Lynn's radical faith was that Jesus had given all of his disciples authority to heal—not through magic but through what she called "the simple gift of presence."

Lynn, who'd been a nurse before she was a priest, had a no-nonsense manner and an impossibly warm heart. "God," she'd pray before sending me and the others off to visit the sick, "comfort us as we need comfort, and kick us in the butts when we need it, and let us show your love to everyone we meet."

Lynn's analysis of healing was straightforward. In an issue of the journal of the San Francisco Medical Society devoted to healing and religion, she wrote:

> As hard as we try to stay healthy, sooner or later we'll all get sick. The bottom line is that we'll die. Acute illnesses can be cured, but some of us live with chronic illnesses. My own relapsing-remitting Multiple Sclerosis, after almost twenty years, is becoming more progressive. I often preach about the impact it has on my life. I also preach about the gifts it has brought me. That is not to be Pollyanish about suffering. To be blunt, suffering sucks.

> Being in the presence of someone's suffering for which you can do nothing provokes an almost universal reaction: the desire to run away as fast as possible. It is frightening to be with someone who is suffering and to feel helpless in the face of anguish and uncertainty.

> Being part of a pastoral care community means learning to be with those who are suffering even when you feel helpless. I believe we are not helpless. We can be beacons of hope

and light for one another, holding the faith that God is at work even when we can't see how. Just knowing you are not alone makes all the difference in the world.

As anyone knows who's been sick or disabled, there are all kinds of extramedical explanations for what illness means—most of them unhelpful. In Jesus' time, the sick were frequently understood to be undergoing punishment for sin, and were shunned as unclean. In some early Christian communities, the ill were anointed as a special "order," and reverenced as icons of the suffering of Jesus. In other periods of history, sick people have been seen, variously, as possessed by demons, as powerful shamans, or as abstract "cases" to be studied. Sick people are often blamed for bringing on their illness through negative thinking or lack of faith or bad habits.

I could see obvious dangers to setting sick people aside as a class at all, whether it was to stigmatize them as failures or romanticize them as special. It felt creepy, just as when middle-class Christians fetishized "the poor," making them into symbols instead of allowing them to be real people.

But I still believed that followers of Jesus had a lot to offer the broader culture—including medical culture— about the kinds of honest relationships the sick could have with the well. There was always a strong tendency among the (temporarily) healthy and able-bodied to want to separate themselves, physically or emotionally, from those who were disabled and ill. By contrast, Christian healing was about simply being together. It meant trusting that illness and suffering were, in the end, just part of our lives—a part that, like anything else, could help bring us closer to God.

Over the years, I'd worked as a volunteer with Lynn, absorbing the values and practical lessons of healing in this context. We weren't doing pastoral care with the expectation that we could fix everyone's problems or end sorrow. Though we understood there were medical and psychological dimensions to pastoral care, we didn't pretend to be doctors or psychologists. Our focus was on presence and spiritual support; and because we were following Jesus, the Word made flesh, a lot of that spiritual work was grounded in plain old bodies. We shared bread and wine; we dabbed oil on foreheads; we carried the weak, held the sad, and rubbed the feet of the dying.

Then Lynn became too sick herself to keep working. I asked Paul if the next pastoral care director needed to be an ordained person. "No," he said thoughtfully. "I don't see why." We were driving down a steep hill toward the church, and I remember thinking I might be about to fall off. I jumped.

"You could hire me," I suggested. "Hmm," he said.

I took the job, and spent time talking with the members of the pastoral care team, figuring out what we were doing. Many of the caregivers were people, as Scripture says, "acquainted with grief"; their qualification came from their own experiences with illness, disability, addiction, or loss. A few had backgrounds in psychology or family therapy. But most, like me, were simply drawn by the Boyfriend, who without any ceremony had given a bunch of fishermen and housewives authority to anoint, heal, and cast out demons.

Cheryl Hendrickson, a hilarious and passionate young teacher, was one of them. Cheryl had trained with Will Hocker at the General Hospital to be a chaplain—not, she explained, because she wanted to work in a hospital. "Ew," she said, waving her hand with a campy, Barbie-doll gesture. Her nails were bright pink, matching the beads on her sandals. "Ew, hospitals are gross." But Cheryl wanted to get better at her painful work of teaching kids in trouble, and thought she'd find clues among the chaplains. "You know," she told me, "I'd randomly enter an ICU, and not know who I was going to meet."

She wrote her story in the same journal that published Lynn's reflections. One day, Cheryl reported, she met the mother of a boy, Leon, who'd been shot in the back of the head and was unconscious. Cheryl said the woman had asked if she had kids of her own. No, she'd said, ashamed.

> I started to wonder what I could do for the mother. I could've stayed and try to fix things, telling her that God was working a purpose out. Or something cheesy like, "God needs Leon up there." I didn't know Leon.

> I could have left the room, giving the mother time to be alone with her son. That would've been easy. I could have left the image of tubes, breathing machines, and loss behind.

There was a third option: staying and being. This meant I needed to sit with my own fears of losing a family member, and sit with the fear that as a childless chaplain I was inadequate.

So I stayed with the mother and I just said, "This has to be so hard." She looked to her son and she cried and I did not leave. I did not leave, and I was uncomfortable.

There was nothing I could do but be with the uncomfortable feelings and believe God was present in that space. In a space that was very close to the ground, very unadorned.

An unadorned space . . . and the temptation always is, as Cheryl noted, to adorn it with cheerfulness, or hope, or even religion. But healing depends on the truth. Jesus, in stark contrast to the airbrushed fantasy of a happy ending promoted by many Christians, offers that truth by simply promising us *life, abundant.* Real life, that is, abundant with awfulness and unbound edges; real life, even with its end.

I wound up praying a lot with people who were dying themselves, or whose beloved friend or husband or mother was ill. I got asked to pray for successful surgeries, for the safe delivery of a child, for recovery from cancer or depression or heart disease. I sat with weeping parents wondering if God would let their baby live. I took a little jar of oil to the pantry and offered healing prayer, listening to stories of lame legs, skin diseases, and blindness that could rival Scripture in their urgent physicality.

And what I learned, among other things, is that prayer does not cure tuberculosis or Down syndrome. Prayer does not cure mental illness. Prayer can't even cure a common cold.

And so, when these things happen, we all rage and weep: What good is prayer? Why did God do this to me? Why do I deserve cancer, when I'm a nonsmoking vegetarian and practice positive thinking? Why did my mother have a stroke, when she worked hard her whole life and never hurt anyone? Why did my baby die? Why, as the people in the Gospel ask Jesus, is this man blind? Is it his own fault, or his parents' fault? Who is being punished?

The Boyfriend shrugs off our desire to establish supernatural cause and effect, to scapegoat and assign blame for illness, to regulate human suffering by formulas that will explain how the good people can be protected. "Neither this man or his parents sinned," says Jesus, patiently. "He was born blind so the works of God could be revealed in him."

Jesus' answer, I fear, is the answer to all the questions of our lives. Sickness, war, falling in love, going to the grocery store: *everything* happens so that God's works might be revealed. But it's up to us to pray—to keep our eyes open—if we're to discover what that means.

Prayer can't cure. All prayer can do is heal, because healing comes embedded in relationship, and prayer is one of the deepest forms of relationship—with God and with other people. And through relationship, there can be healing in the absence of cure.

This is the work that Jesus gives his followers. It isn't about turning ordinary humans into miracle workers who say magic words over a sufferer and restore the sick to perfect health. The power and the responsibility Jesus gives all of us are more frightening: we are, he says, to know the truth, and from that ground enter into new relationships of healing.

Healing—which, basically, hurts like hell.

And which takes a long time.

And which is hard for everyone around you.

I remember when I was working as a cook and had been burned, quite badly, all over my right foot and leg. I had to literally scrape the dead tissue out of the wounds daily for six weeks. Day after day I'd debride my foot, crying. As it healed and nerves came back, it hurt even more—unexpectedly, unfairly. And there was nothing to do but go forward, through the pain, as new flesh emerged.

I remember when my best friend Douglas got sober. It was as if the alcohol and drugs had been a protective jacket around him, and now he was naked: jumpy, prickly, weepy, shivering with exposure. I couldn't stand his new, "healed" self. I was resentful of the work I'd have to do to forge a different kind of friendship with this changing person who seemed to have lost his sense of humor. He didn't like our old jokes; he didn't want to go dancing at our old haunts; he wasn't my reckless, hilarious companion in adventure anymore. I was relieved that Douglas wasn't blacking out, but his healing was a real drag.

"Stop it," I'd snap, when Douglas offered some fresh insight about what he now liked to call my co-dependent behavior. "Don't use that stupid AA jargon on me."

I remember meeting gay people who'd been healed by telling the truth, by coming out. But then they couldn't let go of the suffering that had defined them for so long. They wanted to cling to their familiar identity as victims, blaming and resenting the straight people who'd hurt them. Or they'd insist that their own goodness had saved them, that they weren't like others—those adulterers, trannies, unmarried or promiscuous queers.

But Jesus brushes all our differences away. He is, after all, healing us into himself, dragging us alongside all the other damaged, undeserving people into his body. Healing with Jesus isn't New Age-y and gentle. It is frequently about pain: which might explain, I realized, why Jesus often asks the desperate people who come to him, *Do you want to be well?* Do you want to be well if getting well hurts? Do you want to be well if it separates you from your old identity? Do you want to be well more than you want to stay the same?

Real healing means, more than anything, following the truth: and thus a call to change and conversion.

And anyone can do it. You don't have to be a saint or a professional; there is nothing special, I was beginning to see, about responding to a call to join Jesus in healing yourself and others.

I watched the conversion of my friend Lawrence Chyall, a maitre d' and sommelier who'd helped me launch the food pantry years back. Lawrence was tall and urbane, with a biting wit and a taste for fine Alsatian wines; he was also a fervent Christian, who alternated worshipping at St. Gregory's and an Eastern Rite Catholic Church.

I'd lost track of Lawrence for a few months; a friend told me he was helping a well-known restaurateur open a new place on the waterfront. But when he finally called, it was to say he was applying to nursing school.

"Wow, how's it going?" I asked. I knew the program he mentioned was incredibly competitive, and that older students without medical backgrounds found it hard to get admitted. "What're you going to say when they ask why you're changing careers now?"

"Well," Lawrence said. "What I really want to tell them is: I'm on a mission from God." He cackled.

"Like, how about: there are patients that need their asses wiped, need somebody to listen to them, need somebody to keep the resident physicians from killing them, need somebody to ensure that they get adequate pain meds despite the fact they're junkies. My religion teaches me that these people are united to me through the body of Christ and that they are icons of God's Holy Uncreated Light. So I thought I might do something radical with the remainder of my life and act according to this teaching."

I laughed. "Hmmm," said Lawrence. "You think maybe a slightly more conservative approach might prove more useful?"

But my wife, Martha, was also in the process of changing careers, leaving journalism, and she wanted to become a nurse, too. She had no explicitly religious rationale for it. She couldn't fully explain it. And almost without exception, all of her friends responded in the same way: with an incredulous *"You?"*

Martha's squeamishness was legendary. I'd done my share of accompanying Martha to the doctor for her routine checkups. "Um, I'm not really good with needles," she'd say, as the nurse prepared a draw. Then she'd pass out. Or our daughter would run into the kitchen with a scraped knee, and Martha would go pale. "I have to sit down," she'd say, and stumble to a chair and put her head between her knees.

Martha had always done other kinds of service. She'd mentored screwed-up teenagers, and didn't mind dealing with their abusive parents or advocating with bureaucrats. She didn't hesitate to track down her girls if they ran off to a drug dealer's apartment. But she would never, she swore, bandage up a cut finger.

And then one summer our family went for a month to Nicaragua, where I had lived and worked nearly fifteen years before. I was working on a book; our bilingual daughter was interning at a nonprofit; and Martha, between writing projects, was studying Spanish. It was difficult for her to see the poverty and desperation all around us. "You watch this parade of suffering go by every day," she said, "but we're foreigners; we're not really in it."

We spent one weekend in the mountain town of Matagalpa, trying to escape the stifling heat of the capital, Managua. Driving back toward the city, we started to pass dozens of cattle trucks filled with people instead of animals, so overloaded that men were hanging off their sides. We slowed down at a bend in the road, and all of a sudden we were in the middle of a great throng of shouting men. A guy with his shirt off was waving wildly, and others stumbled toward us, bearing a limp, bloody body in their arms, raising him up high so we could see.

As I halted our tiny rental car and jumped out, I realized they were carrying a man about nineteen or twenty years old. He was unconscious; his face, head, and torso were covered with blood. He had fallen off a truck onto the highway; the driver, afraid of trouble, had just taken off. And the men were handing the body to us: we weren't foreigners or spectators, just human beings who might possibly help. "I'd been riding along, thinking it was so amazing to travel, to see how other people live," Martha told me later. "The next minute it wasn't about *their* lives, but all of ours. They pulled us into the same moment."

I looked at Katie, fifteen years old, ashen in the front seat. I looked at Martha, horrified in the back. "Get him in the car," I yelled at the men. They laid the boy on Martha's lap, his legs bent randomly, his arms dangling, and she took his head in her hands. "Is he still breathing?" I asked. Martha just nodded.

There was something wet on his chest—brains, or vomit—but I couldn't see any place where blood was pumping out. "Tilt his head a bit so he doesn't choke." That was the sum of the emergency first aid I could remember.

I didn't know where to go for help. Matagalpa was two hours behind us; Managua at least an hour ahead. We'd passed a small village about fifteen miles before, and I prayed it might have a doctor or a pharmacist or someone who knew first aid or at least had a telephone. I knew there was a gas station, so I turned back.

"He's still breathing," said Martha, in a thin, flat voice.

She held up the young man's head, as her skirt and T-shirt darkened with blood. "I just thought, oh God, he has a mother," Martha said later. "If he had any consciousness at all he must have been so scared and wanted his mother." So she kept talking quietly to him—in English—telling him to keep breathing, that everything was going to be OK, that she was there.

She stroked his chest. If he's dying, she thought, then I want the last thing he feels to be somebody taking care of him.

We lurched and hit a pothole. Katie gasped. "He's not breathing right," Martha said, panicky. "He sounds like he's choking."

"We're almost there," I said. I had no idea where we were.

Then in a minute we were at the store with the gas pumps. I ran in and begged the woman to tell me where the closest hospital was. "Managua," she said. "What about the Red Cross?" I asked. "A clinic, a doctor?"

No, she said, nobody, but there was a police outpost down the road. I raced the car over a pile of brush, through some mud. We pulled up, honking, at a one-room stucco house where three young men in uniform were standing in the doorway.

There was no station, no vehicles, no first-aid experts, in fact nothing but one desk and a dusty typewriter. One of the cops began to put on a green cotton vest—it said POLICIA on the back—and Katie yelled that a man was dying. It didn't seem to register. He took the vest off, turned it around so the letters were on the front, looked at it and sighed.

"He needs help, he's not going to live, he won't make it all the way to the city," I pleaded to a policeman. He took out a cell phone. Martha leaned out the car window and called to me. "I think I'm going to pass out," she said.

I helped the cops pull the young man out of the backseat. I couldn't remember the word for "spine," so I kept saying *cuello*—watch his neck, please don't move his neck, be careful of his neck. He was still and damp, and his soft lips were slightly open. I realized we didn't know his name. A pickup truck from a neighboring village pulled up, and with great heaving and shouts he was loaded onto the flatbed, and the truck lumbered away.

Katie and Martha came over to me and the policemen, standing in the dust. "Excuse me," Katie said, numbly, in her polite Spanish, "she has to wash her hands; can you tell us where the bathroom is?" She led Martha where the cop pointed her, to an outdoor cement sink with a hose in it, and Martha slowly splashed the tepid water over her bloody arms. We all stood there for a minute, holding on to each other, and then we got back into the car and drove home through the gathering dusk.

It rained that night, a sudden thunderstorm, and heat came up in waves from the hard pavement outside our house. Two days later, Katie read in the newspaper that a man had died from injuries sustained from falling off a truck on the road to Managua.

"Is this our guy?" Katie asked.

"I don't think we'll ever know," said Martha. "But I will always remember him."

So I hadn't been entirely surprised, in the years following that trip, when Martha began talking about nursing school, and then enrolled in night classes at a local community college, studying statistics and pharmacology. She still couldn't stand the sight of blood. But she knew where she was going.

What it took to be a healer, I could see, wasn't necessarily skill, though God knows skill helped. It wasn't necessarily fearlessness, though fear, like disgust, tended to ebb away in the face of the truly interesting new thing. It had something to do with gratitude, a giving over to love.

Will Hocker knew this. "Look what I get to do," he said, happily, surveying the scene at the emergency department. Lawrence knew this. "I just want to hang out with Jesus," he said, rather drunkenly, one evening on my back porch. "And all his dirty pals." And Martha, by the time she gazed inside the flayed torso of a cadaver for the first time, was completely clear. "I've got an amazing, wonderful life," she said. "I want to have more of it. And I want to give more of it."

Martha would become an RN and wind up working at the General Hospital in a wound clinic, "making peace with pus," as one of her friends cheerfully put it. She'd come home and tell me about the patients and their families and the other staff members, marveling at the ordinariness of compassion. "You know," she said once, "you get a homeless patient covered in sores, and his leg's literally rotting, and somebody always just pats his shoulder and says, 'Oh, that must hurt,' and takes care of him. Like it's not a big deal."

"Is it a big deal?" I asked.

"Of course not," said Martha. "It's just that I used to think it would be so hard." She laughed. "Oh, I have to tell you about this man I met today—I've got such a crush on him."

"Really," I said. Katie, who was sitting next to us, looked curious.

"Yeah," said Martha. "He was this huge black guy, really fat, and he stank."

"Oh," said Katie, archly. "Your type."

Martha continued. "Yeah, he smelled awful. And he'd had a stroke, so one side of his face didn't work, and it was hard to understand him, and he drooled."

"Now I get it," said Katie. "Drooling, *totally* irresistible."

"Here's the thing," said Martha. "He just laughed so hard when he'd tell me a joke. Stupid jokes, like he said he wore size fifteen shoes, but he was one of those people who bends over double when he laughs, and even if it isn't funny it's catching. We both kept getting the giggles."

Martha's experience showed me that squeamishness and fear of contagion aren't immutable. But neither are they always connected with clinical illness, or based in the frank fact of messed-up bodies. Often, and especially in religious contexts, the stumbling block for healing is "uncleanliness," where the presence of certain kinds of people threatens the whole social order.

This was the more complex dynamic I could see at work in Christian churches, like my own Anglican Communion, struggling with whether to allow queer people into the body. Some leaders forthrightly declared homosexuality unclean, "an intrinsically disordered condition." For many, that meant excluding "unrepentant" gays entirely, or, with tortured legalism, allowing them to come within a specified distance, but no closer, unless they lied and said they were straight.

But increasing numbers of gay Christians refused to accept the religious authorities' pronouncements. We testified that Jesus had already touched us, claimed us as an integral part of his body, and told us to follow him back into the restored community of all his people. "In his flesh," as St. Paul said, "he has broken down the dividing wall between us, that he might create in himself one new humanity through the cross."

How surprising, after all, to imagine that our divided churches could be healed by the cross. Not through a discourse of "rights," or arguments about who was deserving, but by heading straight to the worst place anyone could be, that place of shame which St. Paul knew was a scandal to decent people. By embracing whatever criminals and thieves we found there, and giving up our hope that we'd be spared by pretending we didn't know them.

The cross erased distinctions. It allowed me to admit that I was an irrational Jesus freak, a sister to fundamentalists, even when I was among my smart, skeptical, secular friends. It allowed Martha to discover that a random stranger's smelly sores were actually less the point than his laughter. It allowed the young straight couple at our church to refuse legal marriage as long as their gay friends couldn't get married, and instead just ask the church to bless their unofficial union.

By welcoming the scandalous, we could be healed of pride: we could admit that our ways were not God's ways. By willingly submitting ourselves, gay and straight, to *be* the scandal, we could be healed of bondage to the law, and start feeling what it was like to live in freedom. A kind of collective sight could be restored, and we could begin to see even the most outrageous, impossible other as Jesus saw us all: weak, sinful, utterly beloved.

This was what I saw happen in the food pantry, precisely because we didn't try to keep the weirdos out. Almost everyone there was outside the order. There was a murderer and a young man who heard voices. There were people battling cancer and people who'd been poisoning their bodies with drugs for years. There were women who looked like men and men who looked like women and kids whose lopsided faces just looked wrong. There was Big Jim, who was still dying from alcohol, yet, with what I could only understand as grace, getting better.

"OK," Paul reported one afternoon, as the pantry was winding down. "Want to know the most beautiful thing I saw today?"

"What's the most beautiful thing?" I asked. I was pretty proud that we'd just served an unprecedented nine hundred people, giving away not only the standard rice and beans and granola bars but some fabulous watermelons the size of toddlers.

"Um, Big Jim's sitting on the bench outside the church with a little Chinese kid," Paul said. "I went over to see what they were talking about, and Jim had given the kid one of our icon postcards. He was so happy the kid took the card, and he said, 'Look, my friend's holding God in his hand!'"

I peeked outside. They were still there, and the child was feeding Jim bites of his granola bar. Big Jim would take a nibble and make a hungry-lion noise, and the kid would crack up.

Our Jesus-based practice of cleansing and healing was different from so much of what modern church, with its focus on safety and professionalism, felt comfortable with. We defaulted to human touch. We didn't grab or bully or demand physical contact, but we certainly put our hands on each other a lot, across social boundaries.

It felt like that long-ago winter when I'd had the mumps, and all I wanted was to curl up, jaws aching, in my mother's arms. It was like watching Paul quiet a fussy baby by laying him on his broad chest and patting the tiny bundle, slowly. It was like embracing Nina, who lived alone, as she tenderly pressed her hot cheek into mine. Or seeing Edmund, who had the "disordered hair" and torn clothes of a leper from the Bible, guiding an old lady up the stairs with a calming hand.

Susan Kellerman, one of the pantry's board members, had a keen eye for who needed to be touched. "That girl," she said to me once, indicating a short, anxious newcomer with a baggy T-shirt who'd been helping me peel potatoes in the kitchen. "She doesn't let anyone close to her. Do you think she's been abused?" It was true: the girl had a kicked-dog look to her, and I thought of how she'd start apologizing in a great rush if I asked her, mildly, to chop the parsley more finely. If I put a hand on her arm, she'd flinch, barely enduring it.

Susan sighed. "Well, just give her time," she said. "You know, working here will make her better. It always does."

I sought out people to touch me and make me better, too. I wanted the little blond baby sitting with her mother at the bread table to grab my hair and shine her toothy grin on me. I wanted to stick a finger, slick with sauce, in Paul's mouth, and see his face light up as he tasted the cumin. I wanted to see the stout Russian woman—who, when I first met her, railed against the filthiness of homosexuals—striding toward me through the chaos of the afternoon with her arms open, demanding, "Sara! Give me kiss!" Like everyone else, I wanted a community bigger than the one I deserved on my own merits.

I still was terrible at asking for help, though. "Occupational hazard," other pastors told me. I was good at dismissing other people's hesitations, the endless cycle of excuses I heard all the time: *I don't want to bother you. Nobody would understand. Other people have real troubles; my problems aren't serious enough. My problems are too serious; there's nothing anyone can do. I'm embarrassed. I'm OK. Nobody really listens, anyway.*

My own excuses were equally dumb. But they were so embedded in my self-image as a capable grown-up that I almost always chose to keep my problems to myself. It was easy enough to ask John to reach up and light the oil lamps when we were setting up for the service, or Michael to move the altar with me when we were cleaning up after the pantry. But asking for attention, comfort, time, listening, prayers—that made my skin crawl.

And yet, when I could force myself to do it, I saw how getting to the point of asking was an essential part of my healing. As much as I might fantasize that my real friends, my most beloved family members, the best priest or teacher or spiritual director would guess just what I wanted and provide it, the fact was I had to ask. I had to put myself in a place of truth, of admitting that I needed help.

"What do you think I should do?" I'd finally say to Paul. I hated being told what to do.

"Honey, I'm worried," I'd finally say to Martha. I always wanted to be the one who told others not to worry.

"I'm afraid," I'd finally say aloud. "I'm upset. Hold me."

And then, usually, I'd discover—no matter whether the person I asked had the perfect response, whether the help disappointed or delighted—that something had changed. I wasn't alone with myself, with my ingrown desires and denials, with the thing that I'd been stewing about in private. I'd given myself over to a relationship.

Just as the sun had risen one winter morning, I was driving Martha to her AA meeting. The routine was that on her day off she went there, and I went to morning prayer at St. Gregory's. It was a peaceful time before the busy day began. We crested the hill, dog owners moving in silhouette over its red dirt and green grass as if they were walking through the sky.

"Did you ever imagine," I said to my wife, "that you'd wind up *here?*"

The shoulders of the hill were dressed in light, light poured off the rocks, light sanctified the faces of joggers and day laborers and third-grade girls in uniforms.

"Not in a million years," Martha said. She had her hair pinned up, looking like what, in fact, she was: a healthy, friendly, somewhat tired middle-aged nurse. "If you'd told me, in my twenties, this would be my life..." Her voice trailed off, and we held hands.

The unexpected is what believers with a sense of humor like to call a blessing. I'd run around the world looking for adventure, working in revolutions, sharing food with soldiers, sleeping on the ground. *Did you ever imagine you'd wind up here?* I'd followed improbable little footpaths to wind up in a New York basement smoking cigarettes with my Haitian sous-chef, or on a mountain ridge in Bali watching white herons circle over a rice field. I'd kissed strangers, I'd poked my nose into places where I had no business, and, when I was forty-six, expecting just another interesting experience, I'd walked into St. Gregory's. Now I was a church lady wearing a cross around her neck. I'd actually brought a coffee cake to Bible study. *Did you ever imagine you'd wind up here?*

The implausibility of this ordinary morning smacked me in the head: what a miracle it was for me to be on my way somewhere with a purpose. And with Martha next to me in our scruffy car: alive, well—even a healer herself.

She'd lived through family mental illness, violence, and suicide; survived her own anorexia, alcoholism, suffocating depression; endured chronic, painful illness. It had been excruciating for Martha, when we first met, to sit at the dinner table with me and Katie. "I can't really deal with families," she'd told me, angrily.

Who knew what had healed Martha, or healed me, or healed our relationship? I knew it began with truth: those days and nights of intense conversation in which we stopped trying to make ourselves look good or to hide how crappy we felt. Now I could look back and see signposts, but the process had been gradual, rooted in years of undramatic, small events. Breakfast, supper, the day at the grocery store Katie refused to let go of Martha's hand. Tears, kisses, the first time we planted bulbs together. Time and love.

Once a troubled young woman had stayed at our house for a few weeks. "I know that kid," Martha had said, wincing. "I've been there." The girl was way too thin, way too reckless, with a propensity for bad boyfriends; she didn't talk much with us, and slunk in late as if to avoid our family meals and questions. But when she moved on, she left an earnest note on a folded piece of paper. "You two surprised me," she wrote. "I never knew that it could be so much fun to be married and live in a house and have a garden."

I dropped Martha off, watching her greet the other alcoholics who were smoking on the sidewalk outside the storefront meeting room. She waved good-bye, then I saw her take the hand of a middle-aged black man and walk inside.

I remembered Paul telling me how, when he was a kid, his parents had always invited neighbors to Sunday dinner, and that they'd all sit around the table holding hands as they said grace. One of the loneliest guests, he said, had been an elderly widow, and one Sunday, after the prayer, she simply asked, "Can we hold hands a little longer?"

When I got to morning prayer, Julie was already there. The church was quiet, and someone had left an enormous bunch of pink lilies that filled the room with sweetness. We sat in silence, we chanted a psalm, we sang.

"Julie, can you read the Gospel?" I asked. We fumbled for a moment finding the passage appointed for the day, and then Julie stood in her windbreaker holding the book with Mark's spare, strange story. "When Jesus had crossed again in the boat to the other side...," Julie began. She read slowly, as the narratives unfolded and knocked into each other.

The leader of the synagogue comes to Jesus to beg him to lay hands on his daughter, who's desperately sick. But while they're talking, a nameless woman in the crowd, who's been bleeding for twelve years, seeing doctors without hope, impoverishing herself, sneaks up to Jesus from behind. She doesn't know who he is, but she's consumed by a desperate thought: if she can just touch the hem of his clothes, she'll be healed. "And at once," Julie read, "the source of the bleeding was dried up in her, and she felt in herself that she was cured. And at once aware of the power that had gone out of him, Jesus turned around."

When morning prayer was done, Julie glanced at me. "I love it that Mark says he felt the power go out of him," she said. "Like it's just going through him, and he's the conduit."

"Do you ever feel like that?" I asked.

"Ah," she said shyly. "Ahh, sometimes."

Then she shook her head. "Yesterday we had a conference on molar pregnancies," Julie said. "It's when a nonviable embryo implants and proliferates in the uterus, and usually causes uncontrollable bleeding. They can cause women to bleed to death."

Julie said that after the lecture, a resident told a story of working in a rural clinic in El Salvador during medical school. A man had come to ask for help for his wife who was "weak and bleeding." The student went up into the mountains and found a pale woman lying in her hammock, unable to get up. She examined the woman's abdomen and found that her uterus was swollen out of her pelvis with a molar pregnancy; she'd been bleeding for months.

Julie was quiet. "I keep picturing that Salvadoran woman crawling through a crowd reaching for his cloak," she said.

Jesus calls his disciples, giving us authority to heal and sending us out. He doesn't show us how to reliably cure a molar pregnancy. He doesn't show us how to make a blind man see, dry every tear, or even drive out all kinds of demons. But he shows us how to enter into a way of life in which the broken and sick pieces are held in love, and given meaning. In which strangers literally touch each other, and doing so make a community spacious enough for everyone. In which the deepest desires of our hearts draw us to health. *Don't be afraid,* Jesus says: your faith will make you well.

forgiving

Guess what?" Zoe demanded one day, in an accusing tone. A sturdy white woman in her sixties, with short hair and a hearing aid, Zoe tended to lean in close and shout when she talked to people. She described herself as "a tough bird" and seldom bothered with niceties. About a month before, she'd announced that I was going to be her priest and spiritual mentor from now on. "I'm not a priest," I said, wearily. We'd been through this before. "Yeah, but your priest should act like they give a rat's ass about you, and you act like that, so you're it. Ha!" Zoe had said.

Now she insisted on giving me regular spiritual updates: she went to Bible study, she voraciously read every book on religion I gave her, she copied out prayers and memorized them, and she wanted to check in at least once a week.

"Guess *what*!" she said again, urgently. "Hey, I'm telling you, that Jesus dude is sneaky. He just hides in the bushes and jumps out and says 'Hey, it's me!' and then you gotta follow him everywhere."

"Where'd he tell you to go?" I asked. Zoe was not easy, but I loved her.

"Oh, man," she said, shaking her head. "I was sitting in my room, you know, and it came to me..." Her voice dropped. "The mother."

I'd noticed Zoe couldn't bear to use the word "my" to describe her parents; she talked about "the mother" and "the father" as if they were characters in someone else's scary movie.

Zoe shivered. "Suddenly I had this thought that said, what would God want you to do? My brain stopped. I didn't know what to do. I said that prayer you gave me from the Book of Common Prayer.

"And then I heard Jesus. You know the mother died of bone cancer, and it just came to me. I thought, well, she wasn't a very nice person, and I'm not going to forgive everything she did, but I knew she must have suffered a lot. And I had compassion. It's a fucking miracle."

The commission to forgive sins, the commission Jesus gives each one of us, is the hardest thing in the world. As hard as "Love one another."

As one more Christian with a weak faith and a strong sense of my own correctness, I found myself frequently unwilling to forgive the homophobic preacher, the passive-aggressive coworker, the drifter at the food pantry who stole my bike lock, my ex. I found myself unable to let go of the grudges that defined me, or to be loved by the wrong people. I found myself afraid to be Jesus.

In Matthew's Gospel, when Jesus heals a paralytic, he reminds the astonished crowd that it's harder to say sins are forgiven than to tell a cripple to get up and walk. In other words, the cures and the healing are almost afterthoughts, tacked on to the real miracle. The miracle is the truly Spirit-filled act of forgiveness, the same life-giving act Jesus practices on the cross.

When Paul Fromberg, in one of his sermons, wanted to explain why that was so hard, he leaned forward. "I've got a trick question for you," he said to the congregation. "God is merciful and just: true or false?"

"True!" called out half a dozen people. Paul smiled. It was a sunny morning, and Paul's voice was warm and generous.

"False," he said. "God isn't just. God is merciful."

Like squabbling kids in any family, of course all of us yearned for justice. We knew the world wasn't fair, and we wanted God to fix it, punishing the wicked and rewarding the good.

Poor Peter, trying to get it right, comes and asks Jesus how much he has to forgive the brother who won't stop doing wrong. Jesus waves away quantification—not seven, but seventy-seven times, he says. A million times.

Jesus isn't being flip. He knows how his disciples struggle with unfairness. He pours out parables about landowners giving the same to hard workers and slackers, or servants forgiving debts without good cause. Jesus

109

tells his friends not to bother with worship until they've reconciled with each other, and to renounce judgment.

My own temptation, though, was to judge and regulate, rather than love. There was the Friday one of our craziest visitors showed up at the pantry, weeping from physical pain and emotional exhaustion. He lived on the streets and was at the end of his rope: he wanted prayer, he wanted help, he wanted healing. He ranted and shouted and cried for a while, and when he finally said something coherent, it was, "My feet hurt so much."

I took him down to the office, as much to keep him quiet as anything else, and sat him in a chair while I got a wet towel. Then I took off his socks and cleaned up the blisters and bandaged them. It was the oddest feeling, watching my irritation dissipate. He breathed on me.

And then I came back upstairs, and yelled at an old woman who'd snuck in out of turn to get her groceries. In a flash I was righteous: she had broken the rules. She was totally wrong. I didn't have to wash her feet or even be nice to her. I felt justified in excluding her, in withholding forgiveness. And, as the Gospel says, the sins were retained.

But even when I was unable to be merciful, when I'd behaved badly, sometimes I was forgiven, for no reason at all. I got loved a lot, and knew it. That day it was Susan making me laugh even as I bitched about the rule breakers. It was Martha showing up unexpectedly to help out, and Paul—like one of those women who follow Jesus and provide for the crowd—cooking a huge pot of parsnip soup to share. I went outside and cried for a minute, blowing my nose on my apron. I couldn't, after all, codify love and forgiveness or argue them into being. I could just kneel down, weep, kiss. Love and healing and forgiveness poured out in my life unreasonably, and what they demanded of me was so much more than compliance with the law. *You have been forgiven everything,* Jesus told me patiently. *Go and show great love.*

I was a little taken aback, though, when my friend José asked me to show love to a stranger, one of his patients. José was a psychiatrist, and a brilliant one, deeply compassionate. I didn't know what I could add to the care he gave. "Well, Tom's dying," said José, carefully. "He wants to talk to somebody religious about forgiveness."

I rang the bell; Tom's apartment was on a quiet, tree-lined block, and I could hear his footsteps as they descended, very slowly, down the stairs. He led me up to a comfortable living room, and sat wheezing on a couch facing me, knees to knees.

"Can I just tell you?" he asked.

I felt dumb, a fraud. Sure, he could tell me anything he wanted; Tom was clearly going to blurt it all out, no matter what. But I didn't know this man. I didn't have any particular words of wisdom about death to share. What was I supposed to do? I'd talked to Will Hocker about confession, what the Book of Common Prayer calls "the sacrament of reconciliation." Will was firm: only a priest could hear a confession and absolve someone; the rubrics said that laypeople could just offer "assurance of God's forgiveness."

"What's the difference?" I asked.

"There's a difference," said Will. "But it's always good to listen and pray."

So I tried to listen to Tom, though his physical presence was unnerving. The man's skin was an unworldly shade of bluish-gray; he could hardly breathe, and his face was gaunt. But the terror Tom felt, he confessed, wasn't about his worsening illness. He wanted his life to be over, but was afraid God wouldn't forgive him.

"I've done bad things and had bad thoughts about my family," he said. "They did such awful things to me. I've tried to forgive them, but I can't." He blamed them, he blamed himself, he wept. "I'm so scared," he kept saying.

In the bluntest of terms the Gospel tells us that in order to receive God's peace, you have to look upon the one you have pierced. You have to tell the truth about how much it hurts. Tom told me his stories of family conflict and cried for nearly an hour, and then, feeling shy, I took his hands in mine. It occurred to me that I just wanted this man to be able to die. I thought of the Pentecostal commission Jesus gives his disciples: not the one with high-drama tongues of fire or rushing winds, but the one in which he simply breathes on them.

"If you retain any sins, they're retained," I repeated the words of that story. "If you forgive any sins, they're forgiven."

I saw why I couldn't do this alone. None of us has the strength to forgive sins by ourselves: our capacity for mercy is just not big enough. We have to empty out our defended, angry, wounded selves in order to be filled with the power of the Holy Spirit. We have to ask for God's mercy, which is infinite, to breathe into us, inspire us.

"Help," I said to myself, quietly. "Oh, help." So we held hands for a while. "I think we should ask God to do the forgiving," I finally said. "Why don't you just say the names of the people who hurt you, and the people you hurt." Tom wept a little bit more, grabbed my hands tighter, and started calling out names; after each one, he and I said "Lord, have mercy." It was odd to be so physically close to a person on his way out of the world: soon this scratchy green tweed sofa would still be in the living room, Tom's sweatshirt would be washed and folded up, and Tom would be...where? I couldn't imagine. I leaned closer, knowing it wasn't my own breath I blew over Tom's gray, damp forehead. "Peace be with you," I said

In the stories of the risen Jesus, his disciples frequently think he must be a ghost. But he asks them for something to eat, he tells them to feel his side, he puts his hands on them. And then Jesus commissions his disciples, giving them the power to share in resurrection. He does it through breath and touch, through Spirit and flesh. He does it

113

through nasty wounds—because you can't claim new life until you recognize, touch, feel, tell the truth about the hurts of the old one. Until you stop hiding.

At St. Gregory's, whenever we sent someone out into the world or launched the person on a new chapter of his or her life, we practiced one of the oldest forms of blessing. We put our wrists on the person's temples, so we could feel the blood beating in both bodies, and then we'd breathe, blowing lightly over the bent head, incarnating, once again, the breath of the Spirit.

We did this with Zoe. From the time she was born until the time she was thirteen, she'd been crucified: beaten, burned, starved, tied up in an attic, raped and beaten again. Her suffering at the hands of her mother and father was horrific, and when she was finally taken away by the state, she was crucified again. She was shuffled through four foster homes and two county jails, then spent three years locked up in a state mental hospital. She ran away, was incarcerated, ran away, was incarcerated. She took up with a traveling preacher's entourage, and was crucified again when she fell in love with a girl. Zoe went through eleven years of analysis, unleashing her astonishing potential as an artist, painting otherworldly canvases full of alchemical symbols. She hand-lettered an illuminated Book of the Dead written in her own hieroglyphic language; she created intricate beaded icons of saints and beasts and gods; she covered boards with detailed epics. Zoe won a scholarship to a Catholic college, where she soared intellectually, earning two master's degrees, but she'd acquired some scars—including deafness, a profound addiction to alcohol, no money, and persistent mental illness.

Zoe arrived at the doors of our church only partway through a healing process—a process brought about by grace, a gifted and loving therapist, and her fierce desire to stop drinking. She was in terrible shape. Zoe had to be one of the most intelligent people I'd ever met, and one of the bravest. She was also impossible. Getting sober had opened up every wound of her life, everything she'd hidden away, and she would fight with anyone who tried to care for her, raging and weeping and literally bellowing with pain.

Then after a year or so Zoe came to me and said she was ready to let go of the idea of multiple personalities who had accompanied her through the years of crucifixion. She explained that she'd dissociated to protect herself, naming "Scott" as the part of her who served as "keeper of the pain," "Dave" who handled the wounds, "Margie the religious freak," and on and on. She showed me what she'd painted: a small, trippy, multicolored icon, with a stylized image of each personality. In the middle was the figure of her new self, Zoe, walking forward into the light, holding the hand of someone who looked like a cross between her therapist and Jesus.

"I want you to keep this in a safe place," Zoe said, awkwardly. "It's like my birthday today; I'm going to start just as me."

I stood with her by the outdoor baptismal font, holding the icon, as she touched each figure and told me, in excruciating detail, the stories behind them. Zoe and

115

I blessed the icon, and, as she would put it later, "gave my personalities over to the care of God." It was a windy afternoon, and there were birds darting around the water.

I put my wrists on the sides of her head and reached over with my thumb, making the sign of the cross, trying not to cry. I breathed on her, speaking aloud her single name.

"Zoe, you have the power to forgive sins," I said. "Go in peace."

"Just breathe," people would say sometimes, trying to calm me down. It was kind of annoying. Who could forget to breathe? But I could easily forget the peace I'd passed, just breathing, to Zoe or to Jim, and instead find myself overwhelmed by what I imagined were the demands of love.

There was a tradition at St. Gregory's among the people who led worship on Sundays. Before the service, even before we began to arrange chairs and get the oil lamps lit, we'd gather in the seating area and pray. "Blessed be God the Word," we'd chant, "who came to his own, and his own received him not, for in this way God glorifies the stranger."

Out of the corner of my eye, I'd see one more person I didn't want to deal with heading toward our group with a determined look: *There's a man asking for spare change outside; I can't find the key to the back gate; hey, do we have any Band-aids?*

"Oh God," we'd finish, "show us your image in all who come here today, that we may welcome them, and you."

But I didn't want to see Jesus in every parishioner: the whiny woman who complained endlessly about the music, or the sullen, depressive guy who was rude to visitors. I didn't want to welcome him in every single visitor, either: I got so crabby about the way clergy, in particular, presumed I'd always be available and overflowing with generous attention.

Once, after church, after two services and eighteen conversations, after we'd finished washing the dishes from coffee hour and I'd given the last crumbs of communion bread to the birds, after I answered the last questions from curious visiting youth groups and listened to the last unhappy member confess the wreck of her home life, I went and found Paul, who was cleaning up the Sunday School room.

"Aren't we even allowed to have lunch?" I asked. "Enough church. Your Boyfriend is wearing me out. I cannot deal with one more human being."

"What about the French place?" said Paul. The café down the street served a great aioli with its salty, crisp fries. I couldn't wait to sit down and order a hamburger.

At the corner, two homeless men, deep in conversation, passed by. One was bearded, wearing a filthy down jacket, and he looked up and nodded at us. "Hi, Sara," he said.

"I don't know that guy," I said.

Paul shot me a glance. "God's messing around with you," he said.

God didn't need me to take care of everybody, or radiate sweetness all the time. God didn't need my ridiculous overdeveloped conscience. God just needed me to recognize Jesus, whenever he showed up and said hi.

Because when Jesus showed up, even the most painful moments held something I could rest in. There existed, as the old hymn said, "streams of mercy," and they often flowed right alongside suffering. One afternoon, I'd gone to join a peace march organized by parents and others in my neighborhood in response to the recent murders of six people. Some of the victims were gang kids, some drug dealers, some random bystanders. I lived just a block and a half away from where two of the victims were shot, and I knew how many other teenagers were caught up in a cycle of revenge. I brought an icon of Mary holding her infant son, with a note taped to it that read, "We're all children of God. May God forgive us all, that we might forgive each other."

There were about a hundred people standing together on the corner, preparing to walk the stations of suffering, past every site of a murder. I heard plenty of stories about the gangs: how they rule by terror, how they're chased by the cops, how they bring in juveniles from other poor neighborhoods in the Bay Area to sell drugs and kill people.

I talked with a frightened mom and her daughter, who told me they ran out of their house when they heard the gunfire that destroyed two boys, to try to help, but it was too late. I prayed, alongside some white hipsters and an entire Salvadoran family, at a homemade street shrine for one victim. His kids had left a crayoned sign on the curb that read: "Papí we miss you." I talked with a sad-faced Latino guy who taught math in a middle school, who just kept saying, "The politicians want to have a curfew and put all our kids in jail. Doesn't the word *mercy* mean anything?"

I thought of that math teacher when, a few weeks later, I drove up to Juvenile Hall to accompany a beloved parishioner whose kid was being tried for possible felonies. The boy wasn't violent, but he'd always been deeply troubled. Now fifteen, tall and fair, his face still looked childish.

His parents had adopted him as an infant. His mother, a slender woman with pale Irish skin, had accompanied him through years of special education and testing and tutors and psychologists, trying to find him help. Her husband and their other son had brought him to baseball games and Boy Scout camp, advocated with teachers, shaped the family's life around his needs. I'd met the boy when he was only ten, a mop-headed, solidly built child with incredible energy who loved going to church, and who couldn't hold still for five minutes of it.

119

I sat there on the waiting room benches, and all I could think about was the "hard wood of the cross," as Christians say.

It is *really* hard. It's hard to have to hold the ways we hurt and fail each other. It's hard to hold betrayal, and loss, and the violence and emotional pain that people inflict on their families and strangers. It's hard to bear the weight of the principalities and powers that bind our lives: the crushing, unfair justice system, the courts, the "machine," as this boy's mother said to me. "It's like he's going slowly down into the mouth of a machine that's going to swallow him up."

The cross is just plain hard.

As is the good news of Jesus, which tells us that suffering is real and that joy comes in the morning. That the humiliation and pain of the cross—of watching a disturbed child suffer, of having a kid in jail, of wishing but being unable to stop violence—is always, everywhere, redeemed by love.

I sat on a bench in the shabby little Juvenile Hall courtyard with the mother and her lawyer, and we prayed. The words of the psalms we chanted aloud—"Lord, remember not the transgressions of my youth"; "the valley of the shadow of death"—these words hung there, accompanied by the shouts of incarcerated kids, the banging of windows, the smokers' conversations, the clatter of feet going up and down the stairs to judgment.

Later we stood together outside the courtroom, and the boy, his hands cuffed behind him, bent his head down.

"Mom," he said, "could you scratch the back of my neck?" The guard moved aside, and she touched her son.

God knows our lives are hard, and God knows we make them harder all the time through obdurate, judgmental actions; through faithless reliance on law; and through vain refusal to participate with Jesus in mercy.

But God's mercy remains everlasting. It's wide. It's profligate, encompassing devastated victims, ashamed parents, kids who've been hired to kill other kids, and adults who've been hired to handcuff and guard children. It encompasses me, with my prideful and inarticulate desire to make a difference; it encompasses the neighborhood woman who failed to save a life; it encompasses the saintly math teacher and the angry gang leader. It holds the judge, the betrayer, the condemned criminal, and Mary, the criminal's mother, in perfect love.

Zoe had stayed sober, and found a place to live, and begun coming to church regularly, but she was wracked by doubt. How could there be a God, she said, who'd allow such terrible things to happen to her? How could Jesus be real? She would periodically call me up in a rage about her family as the memories of violence got clearer and clearer. I remember one phone call when she threatened to, as she put it, "break up with God."

"Jesus says love your mother and father," she shouted, "and I can't do that. That's *wrong* what they did to me. I was just a little kid. I can't be a Christian if I have to forgive them. That's *wrong*!" And then she'd cry and cry.

All we could do was touch her. I'd deliberately put a hand on her when we talked, I'd drape an arm around her, I would sit too close at lunch.

All we could do was feed her. "Hey, where's the beef?" Zoe demanded once, bursting into the kitchen where Paul and I had been cooking for the food pantry volunteers. She was holding out a plate with some mashed potatoes and coleslaw on it, and complaining loudly. "I got here late, and there's no meat left. Everybody else got meat." Paul, who like all cooks ate standing up, just speared the piece of brisket from his plate and put it on hers. "Here you go," he said.

"Nah," she said. "Nah, that's yours, I didn't mean..."

"Workers gotta eat," said Paul.

All we could do with Zoe was give her work to do caring for others. We asked Zoe, just like the rest of our broken, hurting volunteers, to lift sacks of potatoes and put bread on tables and offer food to everyone. We asked her to sweat and get a sore back and talk to people she didn't know. We asked her to give her hands and her back and her heart away. And to tell the truth.

The truth is that suffering can become the foundation of faith, if we're not scared to touch the sore places with love. If we don't hide ourselves away in fear, but get close enough to others to feel God's breath on our skin. Everything that hurts the body of Christ can let us know, past doubt, that new life is possible—not by forgetting evil, but through, in terms that are both religious and secular, truth and reconciliation.

One day, about a year after giving over her icon, Zoe came to me and said, "I don't *want* to forgive them. But I want to be free. I'm sick of carrying the parents around." She wiped her eyes. "It's rough," she said. "I don't know what to believe. I'm just exhausted. I want to have a new life."

"You are already in it," I said.

So I went to Paul, and he prepared a ceremony for Zoe. It wasn't a baptism—she'd been baptized by her parents as an infant, and we weren't going erase the past and pretend it didn't exist.

Instead, we asked her to affirm her baptismal vows aloud, in celebration. It had been a painful year—a year of being sober, a year of living with truth, and a year of struggling to forgive. It was an unfinished year, because our lives are unfinished work.

We stood close around the altar, in the middle of the empty room, touching each other. "Will you continue the apostles' teaching and fellowship, in the breaking of bread, and in the prayers?" asked Paul, reading the vows of baptism, his voice deep and slow. I could hear some kids laughing in the playground, and trucks backing up into the loading zone next door.

"I will," said Zoe, "with God's help."

"Will you seek and serve Christ in all persons, loving your neighbor as yourself?" "I will," Zoe said, "with God's help."

I kept my hand tight on her shoulder, and our breaths rose and fell together. Paul blew over her wispy gray hair. When we were done praying, we shared little glasses of milk that, adapting an ancient church practice, we'd set out on the altar with spoons of honey. "So that the first thing in your new life will be sweet," Paul explained.

Then Zoe went out, and Paul and I washed up the glasses, and started talking about other things we had to do at work, and went back to our phone calls and meetings. Afterwards, walking up to the deli for a sandwich, Paul stopped and turned to me, and said, quietly, on the sidewalk, "Death has no power at all."

raising the dead

The promise of the resurrection is that Jesus has not only risen but destroyed death itself. He has overthrown death, trampled it down, and he forever hauls all the rest of us out of our tombs. As St. John Chrysostom wrote in the fifth century, "Death swallowed a body and met God face to face.... Death has no power any more."

But of course death, and the fear of death, continue to drive so much on earth. They lie under all human violence, drive our sad struggles for domination, allow the manipulations of religion and empire to thrive. As a war reporter, surrounded by terror, I'd experienced the power death had to make me betray or refuse to help others. I'd seen people who were, in their souls, no more than walking dead: they were completely ruled by fear of the grave. I believed in my own churning guts, those mad days and nights, that violence was the real force driving the world. Death seemed unstoppable.

And yet I witnessed amazing sights, as well, whenever a person left the fear of death behind, and rejected the temptations of power through violence. I saw unarmed civilians walk straight into a line of sharpshooters. I saw a mistreated woman let go of revenge, and instead offer a stranger a cup of tea. I saw a scared kid refuse to strike a prisoner. These people had a totally different kind of power, one which comes from believing that death doesn't have the final word.

It had been a long time since I'd been afraid someone would kill me. But I knew how much I still hesitated to put myself on the line to risk hurt, or even inconvenience, social embarrassment, the disapproval of authorities. Once, visiting another city, I'd been cutting through a desolate part of downtown—boarded-up buildings, windowless office buildings, a few dingy liquor stores. It was cold, with freezing sleet, and all I wanted was to get back to my warm hotel, and then I heard shouting. Half a block away I saw two police cars pull up, and a group of cops yelling at a guy curled up in a doorway. I took a step toward them and stopped. One of the cops looked up and waved me away, and I turned back and moved on. Afraid.

But Christ, crucified, has come to sweep away that fear. The power to reject and hurt and kill is shown by Jesus as, finally, irrelevant, in the face of the power to love so unreservedly that you gladly pour out your life for others. God's weakness turns out to be stronger than human strength. Even death is over. As Jesus says, on the cross: *it is finished.*

"Proclaim that the Kingdom of Heaven is at hand," Jesus tells his disciples, before he goes to his end, instructing them to go forth and raise the dead. "You've received freely, now give freely."

Of all the things I thought I heard Jesus telling me to do, raising the dead was the most impossible to take literally. The resurrection was a logical sticking point for those who didn't accept Jesus as divine, and even for many believers it had become merely a metaphor or a statement about principles. But I believed it: other things I'd thought of as metaphorical turned out to be real. Communion was food. Healing was touch. When I received love, freely, I wanted to give it away in the same spirit.

Yet what could it possibly mean to raise the dead?

I knew a little bit about new life, because I'd seen it shine in people like Zoe and Martha. I'd even discovered, to my great surprise, some new life of my own, albeit mixed up messily with leftovers from the past, surprising me: *Did you ever imagine you'd wind up here?*

In my new life with the Boyfriend, I wasn't particularly nicer, but I was freer. I wasn't more holy, but I felt more blessed. And I knew that to the extent new life was real, in any of us, it had sprung, just as Jesus promised, from actual feeding, healing, forgiving. It didn't come from the sky, but from plates of enchiladas, the bruises of strangers, frustration and tears. *Follow me,* Jesus had said: just give the people something to eat, just touch them, just say you're sorry. And our lives had changed.

But raising the dead didn't seem like work it was possible for humans to do.

"Hi," said the woman on the phone, breathily. "Is this St. Gregory's? Like the food pantry? I saw on your Web site you've got a program called Scared Dying, and, well, I'm dying and I'm scared of dying. So will someone come and pray with me?"

Sacred Dying, a program developed by the writer Megory Anderson, was used by the church to train family members and friends in end-of-life issues and in helping people in hospice achieve a "holy death." But the woman who was calling me had misread the title for a reason: she was, she said, just plain afraid.

"Not so much for myself," she explained when I showed up at her apartment in the wretched housing projects of Potrero Hill. From her chair, Laura surveyed the barred window where a breeze blew through torn leopard-print curtains, and pointed to a school portrait of a boy in a clip-on tie. She was breathing through nasal tubes attached to an oxygen tank, but sipped air by mouth hungrily as well, gasping lightly with each intake, as if she were under water. "When God's ready for me, he'll take me. But my son." Tears rolled over the plastic tubes. "My Gabriel. What will happen to him?"

Over the next few months, I'd learn more about the exceptional determination of Laura, who in fact had less fear—or faced it more directly—than almost anyone I'd ever met. A massive pyramid of a woman with long, curly hair, she was dying of advanced lung cancer ("and," she said, "a lot of other things") and had just been placed in home hospice care. Her fourteen-year-old son, Gabriel, and her sturdy, poker-faced Salvadoran friend, Gloria, were caring for her, taking shifts sleeping near Laura to help with the breathing apparatus and to administer medications. A hospice nurse came by the cramped, stuffy apartment weekly; a couple of neighbors gave Gloria a hand with trips to our food pantry for groceries; and the family dog, a hamster-size Chihuahua named Baby, constantly ran around the sick woman in adoring circles, peeing and squeaking and trying to jump on her lap. "Baby!" Gloria would scold when the dog barked at me. "*Cállete.*" Then she'd bring a glass of water, setting it down carefully in front of us on the broken coffee table, on a folded paper towel.

I didn't choose Laura, any more than I chose Jesus: she chose me, and insistently behaved as if I were going to be part of her solution for her family. And it was hard to resist her. Laura had a radiant smile. She looked right at me whenever she spoke—softly, because she was always struggling to breathe—but in complete, jarringly honest sentences. If, as I had discovered, truth was the prerequisite for healing, then Laura was vibrant with health.

"I have been blessed," she pronounced. "My mother didn't want me to live, and then of course I didn't want to live, but God seems to have wanted me to live. He sent me Gabriel. He was born perfect, strong, and it didn't matter how many drugs I'd done while I was pregnant with him, he was OK, so I decided I was meant to be healed, too."

It had been a long journey to healing. Born on the Indian Ocean to a Goan mother—a self-styled "missionary" with a propensity for beating her children—and a quickly absent Angolan father, Laura was moved to Kinshasa in Congo and then to housing projects on the south side of San Francisco. By the time she was nineteen she was fluent in Hindi, Portuguese, French, Lingala, English, Spanish, and an eloquent Afro-Pinoy-Spanglish mash-up from the projects. She turned to using then selling drugs, and commanded every racket and hustle on the streets with her quick mind and fearlessness. She was beautiful. She was nuts. She took up with a series of more or less hapless men, marrying some of them and simply working the others; she began to drink seriously. By the time Laura was twenty-two she had lost one daughter to the courts, and given birth to a baby who weighed less than a loaf of bread and died within two weeks.

130

The narrative of recovery tends to focus on the one moment in which the addict sees the light or hits bottom or becomes "saved." After Gabriel was born, Laura was dragged to an AA-NA meeting by a friend, but what seems to have saved her was the vision of herself as someone who could save others. She became a fierce warrior, wading into the rushing waters of junkie life to pull her comrades out. "I'd stay up with them all night, praying," she said. "I'd cook for them, I'd find someone who could get them fake papers, I'd take away their guns when they threatened to shoot themselves."

And she decided to become the kind of mother she had yearned for: a toucher, a kisser, a talker. She went to community college and became a peer counselor for alcoholics; went to church and became, to the limits of her strength, a forgiver.

"I used to be a Catholic," she said, "and then I became a Christian. I know everyone believes different things, but the most important thing is love. I try to get over it when people do me wrong."

She made Gabriel do his homework and pray, and she mastered the hard art of asking for help. "My mom didn't know better," Laura told me once, remembering how she'd been whipped with an electric cord and chased out into the streets half naked in the middle of the night for mentioning that she had a boyfriend. "I want Gabriel to know he can always talk to me, and he's not gonna get into trouble if he tells me the truth."

Gabriel was, like his namesake, an angel. Tall, sweet, dark skinned, with a boy's mumbling awkwardness, he bore the stamp of a child who'd been well loved in the midst of a war. Laura had made sure he stayed in touch with his father, a ponytailed Mexican guy, and found him tutors and mentors and "brothers" from their current Pentecostal church, Agua Viva (Living Water). And now she was making sure he'd talk with me.

Gabriel could express his feelings with uncanny precision—"Mom," he said once in my hearing, "I love you so much, but it upsets me that you're going to die, so sometimes I want to fight with you"—and he could rest his head, unselfconsciously, on his mother or on Gloria, though Gloria would smack him and say, "Enough, Gabriel, I love you too, but finish the dishes." Unlike most of the kids in the projects, Gabriel had resisted the corner and gangs; he went to school, to church, and to a church camp, without ever suggesting that he deserved more glamour and excitement in his life. Having a mother about to die was probably enough drama for a fourteen-year-old.

Gloria was opaque. She was the kind of middle-aged woman Central Americans call *cumplida* and *trabajadora*—responsible, hardworking, serious. Short and stoic, she didn't speak English, though she understood enough to communicate with a couple of the black women on the block whom Laura had befriended. I'd talked some with Gloria when she came to pick up groceries at our food pantry, and she was relaxed enough to call me "Sarita," but there was always a reserve. Once, when I brought Paul, in his cassock, to visit the household, she called him Father and hovered at the edge of the conversation like a servant. I knew that Gloria, the only daughter of a provincial officer with nine sons, had served for years in the Salvadoran army, and bore an ugly bullet scar on her forearm; I knew she had crossed over to California alone, at great risk, and stayed without papers or legal status. Gloria had been sponsored in AA by Laura, and welcomed into Laura's church; now, she said, she was returning the favor. "The woman saved my life," she said. "I am going to stay here and take care of her for the rest of her life, whatever she needs."

What Laura needed was hard for me to figure out—not because she was shy about asking, but because I didn't understand how she was thinking about death and resurrection in her final months. Laura had been fed, healed, forgiven. She had fed, healed, and forgiven others. Laura, in fact, believed that she had already been reborn once, just as she had helped Gloria be reborn, by finding a new and sober life. And now she intended to keep herself alive, through Gloria and through her son, even though she knew she was dying.

Every November, our church celebrated All Saints' Day, All Souls Day, and Dia de los Muertos, the feast days for the dead that come clustered together on the calendar. It was always a strange season for me. The days were shorter and the nights colder and longer. And in addition to the public feast days, I marked other personal days of remembrance: the food pantry anniversary, my baptism, the birthday and the death of my father.

Right before his birthday in November 1996, my father had died, unexpectedly. The door between this world and the next just swung open. One moment there was a breathing, eating, human being clothed in flesh: a person in a body, a body I could touch and kiss and hold, and then there was not.

The food pantry launched on another early November weekend, in 2000, around St. Gregory's altar. Two days later, I was baptized at St. Gregory's outdoor font. Without being conscious of it, I'd chosen my father's birthday for the baptism. In that liturgy, called "thanksgiving over the water," I'd vowed to die to my old life and take on a new one.

And now it was November again. As we launched into the weekend of feast days and remembrances, my father was even more on my mind than usual. My uncle Paul—my father's younger brother—had died two days before. Then I'd spent an afternoon at Laura's bedside. I learned that Martha's father was sick. And I was waiting to hear back from a dear friend diagnosed with melanoma. Death was all around me.

But there was also life: and it began with feeding, at the food pantry, as we celebrated the anniversary of our founding. Early in the morning, in a great rush of the Spirit, our volunteers started to blow in: friends and first-timers, people who'd lost old lives and found new ones through sharing this work.

Susan, who'd been part of the pantry for years, stood next to me looking around the bustling rotunda with a huge smile. She and her husband had "plenty of money," she'd told me once. "And so I came here thinking that I was going to help other people. I discovered I was so hungry. For this experience, this life."

"My sister!" said Paul, striding into the kitchen with his hand raised to greet me. "What are we feeding the saints for lunch today?"

We discussed the relative merits of King Ranch chicken and meatloaf for a while, then I left Paul and Susan to start lunch, while I drove to the warehouse of the food bank. Another volunteer, Elizabeth, brought holy oil, and we anointed the hands of the guys who worked there, taking their hands in ours, receiving their blessings and calling down blessings on them. I remembered what one of the floor managers had told me. "At the end of the day," he said, "you're just so thankful, because you got to make sure some folks had dinner."

There were fifty volunteers for lunch, and Paul had made trifle for dessert. After the meal, I got a loaf from the bread table and put it on the altar. Steve Hassett, who'd helped me open the pantry eight years ago, was a priest now; he led everyone around the altar, censing the food and the altar as we sang. Jake, a homeless addict, his face glowing, read the Gospel aloud. "Jesus saw a great crowd," Jake said, hoarsely, "and his heart went out to them."

The afternoon went on, a million stories, a hundred hugs, a dozen languages, hands, food, everyone moving around the altar, in and out the doors, down the street, in the doors, out again. I stuck my hand in the water of the font at one point, where Benny, a taciturn Filipino guy in a baseball cap, was breaking down cardboard boxes. There were three big blue recycling bins, overflowing, and I could see the piles of potatoes by the altar.

I crossed myself with the cool water. "Dad," I thought. It had been eight years of the pantry, eight years of baptized life. I didn't understand how fast it had happened, and wished, so sharply it brought tears to my eyes, that my father could see this. Benny interrupted me. "Sara!" he said. "You want some?" He handed me a bottle of sweet iced tea, and I drank deeply.

That evening I walked through the streets of my neighborhood, past all the homemade shrines for Dia de los Muertos. In the dark park was a circle of tiny babies' shoes arranged on the grass to remember dead children, and bunches of marigolds. Every bodega and grocery store had pictures of ancestors, lit by flickering candles. Throngs of noisy young people filled the street. St. Peter's Catholic Church was open for mass, but outside its doors as well as inside, I saw the one church, the body of Christ.

I wound up late at Anibal's three-room apartment, where he was celebrating a Candomblé All Saints and Souls liturgy. The place was covered floor to ceiling with homemade shrines, and a little picture of Tinkerbell

136

fluttered above the icon of St. Barbara by the door. Anibal laughed when I pointed it out. "All the girls," he said, "all the girls are welcome tonight."

I thought about the disapproval most churches expressed at the very idea of syncretism, yet how much it seemed, in practice, that a living faith mixed things up. Culture, that great human yeast, continued to rise and swell and sour the flesh-and-blood experience of God in every time and place.

Catholics could scorn Candomblé, and Muslims scorn Catholics, and Anglicans scorn the wrong kind of Anglicans, yet so many religious dogmas were basically just accumulations of surviving heresies. Their supposedly eternal articles of faith were frequently piled up one on top of another like the cuisine of Gregory of Nyssa's Cappadocia, or, for that matter, of my own San Francisco: Roman, Turkish, Greek, Indian, Chinese, North African, Egyptian.

Yet all religions, at one point or another in their evolution, tried to proclaim their single, inerrant consistency. All religions, even the most liberal, were tempted by the reactionary impulse to freeze faith in place. Because, as Jesus teaches, it's easy to be threatened by the reality of the complicated, messy, syncretic, God-bearing truth that becomes incarnate among us and makes things new. We'd rather have a dead religion than a living God.

The drumming started: there was no boundary between worship and eating and drinking. "Yeah, we're tacky," said a friend of Anibal's, waving a hand around at the sequined cloths on the altar, the kitschy icons, the tortilla chips. "But God loves tacky, because God loves what's from the heart."

As the liturgy went on, I talked with a woman who'd been "born" to the service of the orishas in Cuba. I met a Buddhist nun who'd taken vows of homelessness and held funerals for people who died on the streets. I swapped jokes with a hilarious unbeliever and shared a coconut shell full of rum that was passed around from hand to hand. Anibal introduced me to one of his Candomblé initiates. "This is Sara," he said. "She's a priestess of Jesus." The man nodded and crossed himself. "Hi," he said.

We chanted and danced and drummed, and then Anibal stood to preach by the balcony outside the living room, where candles flickered in the night before bunches of flowers and icons of the saints.

The door is open, Anibal told the crowd, and God passes back and forth. We're here because of our ancestors, the ones who go before. We know we'll die too, but life itself goes on, God's body keeps breathing, and we are part of that forever. Then he fed us soup.

"There's some regular food too, but this is liturgical food, made from roots," he explained, handing me a bowl of the steaming, thick stew. "Comes from the ground, where we're going. At some point someone else is gonna eat root soup, and there will be little molecules of Sara in it."

I stumbled out into the night, the drummers still raising their chants to the dead. "Hmm," said the Buddhist nun, walking unsteadily behind me. "You know, I think there might have been alcohol in that coconut shell."

It was overcast and rainy when I got to St. Gregory's the next morning to set up for the All Saints' Day service. Mark Dukes, the gifted iconographer of the massive fresco of saints dancing around the top perimeter of the rotunda, had been working on gilding some halos. So when I lit the first candle, I saw a blizzard of gold leaf—little scraps of trimmings in drifts on the floor, caught on the moldings, on the table, everywhere. The gold leaf was so incredibly light and fragile that it was almost impossible to pick up: it blew away with the slightest motion, and crumbled into dust in my hand. But I just had to touch the stuff. I kept kneeling down in the candlelight and trying to sweep up tiny bits of holiness, bits of the halos that had fallen from the saints and were now stuck on the ends of my fingers like a souvenir from God.

But of course the gold hadn't come from heaven. The halos had been applied skillfully with tools by the completely corporeal Mark Dukes, who used his hands to make the connection between the saints above and us below.

The beauty and brightness of the gold wasn't magic. It was real. Like death. Like bread. Like the presence of God.

We all had real bodies. To chew up a piece of bread meant that, like the saints, I was mortal flesh, and sooner or later going to die. But eating that bread or the root soup also revealed me, like all the saints, to be a soul in a body, a piece of God in a piece of flesh.

The absence of my father remained huge, this morning and always. I missed him so much. And yet I couldn't have known how vividly present he would become to me, how I'd keep seeing him in specific articulations of my daughter's being—a crooked pinky finger, the eager tilt of a neck reading. And how, unexpectedly, just walking down the street, I'd be able to glimpse that door between life and death, still open.

And so I shared communion with everyone who'd gone before: my father, strangers, the nameless and forgotten, heroes, and every loopy, unlikely child of God, including my enemies. I ate the body of Christ because all together we—the saints pictured on the icon dancing above and us dancing below—we *were* the body of Christ. We were the body itself and the memory of it. We were the body itself and the promise of it. One body, aflame with little scraps of earthly gold, eating our real bread, surrounded by death, in the face of eternal life.

This wasn't a miracle. Because faith, as I was beginning to see, was hardly a miracle: it was more like living in a different key, being tuned, as the hymn said, to grace. It meant the kind of trust suggested by the story of Jesus walking over the water to a panicky boatload of disciples.

It's night in the story, and stormy, and the frightened fishermen think they see a ghost moving toward them. Jesus, as he likes to do, calls out, "It's me! Don't be afraid!"

Peter replies, "Lord, if it's you, tell me to come to you on the water." So Jesus invites Peter to come, and he gets out of the boat and begins walking on the water toward Jesus. But when Peter takes his eyes off Jesus and sees the big waves, he begins to sink. Peter cries out, and Jesus immediately reaches out his hand and grabs Peter. As they climb into the boat together, the storm stops. "Man of little faith," Jesus says to Peter, irritated, fond, "why did you doubt?"

Laura had faith. But still she worried: that after her death Gloria would be deported, that Gabriel wouldn't be able to stay in the apartment. And sometimes in the darkest hour, in the fourth watch of the night, she feared her son would be lost to the streets, as so many kids up on the hill were. Lord, she said with Peter, save me. She wanted a miracle.

Gloria wanted a miracle, too. She'd already lost so many members of her family to sickness, old age, and violence; she couldn't bear to lose Laura, too. "My queen, my friend, my sister," she called her. "My heart."

It was stormy on that boat. Right before Gabriel went away to summer camp, he'd fought with his mother. They yelled and he stomped out, and didn't speak for a week. But when the boy came home, he'd pushed open the door and said, "Mom, forgive me." And she'd pulled herself to her feet and said, "Honey, forgive *me*." And they'd reached out their hands at once, and held each other, with the waves crashing around them.

"Lord," said Peter, "if it's you . . ." Peter wanted proof; he wanted a miraculous sign.

But the miracle was really just his ordinary, flawed, human willingness to be in the storm, to be scared, and to try to follow Jesus anyway. Like Laura and Gloria and Gabriel, who kept moving, however imperfectly, toward the force calling them to be bigger, braver, and more loving.

Laura had walked with her big ungainly gait straight out of the prison of her illness and grabbed my hand, demanding that I help her family. And her insistence gave me courage: me, who was afraid of the whole mess. Who was afraid of dying, of watching Laura die, of being helpless.

Because little faith, they taught me, is not *no* faith. Little faith is just the oscillating mixture of trust and doubt that's part of being human. The lesson isn't that if we had more faith we could walk on water or that God will reward our great faith with supernatural powers and send the storms of life away.

It's that, as long as we love each other, we aren't alone. "It's me," Jesus says. "Don't be afraid."

The most confusing thing about West Coast slums is how they've got so much sky. The Potrero Terrace projects were laid out on the side of an iridescent green hill, crowned with wide-open sky, its complicated light and sheer immensity always pulling my eyes up, past the wrecked cars and discarded Pampers that clogged the streets. I'd visit Laura and other people I knew from the food pantry there often, and every time I got out of my car at the top of the hill, I'd feel tiny yet exalted, dwarfed by the universe.

In the projects, you could be driving past a clutch of exhausted moms yelling at their kids, and the trembling lavender heavens, stretching across the San Francisco Bay, would shimmer with the presence of a cosmic power. You could start heading down a broken sidewalk, and the rain would begin from on high like a message from prophets. You could be standing at one of the omnipresent corner altars for a dead gangbanger—gazing at a Mylar balloon from Safeway, some soggy teddy bears, cognac bottles, dead flowers, maybe a name and a RIP scrawled on a piece of poster board—and above you, Old Testament clouds and shafts of light would suddenly break open, the sky black and gold and piercing blue by turns, illuminating the memorial trash with its almost unimaginable vastness.

And then you would go inside.

Inside there was no sky—in fact there was no air. Everything felt stale and constricted, not smelling bad as much as hopeless, the air missing some element necessary for breathing. No matter how much someone cleaned, it was impossible to erase the historical accumulation of odor, the olfactory equivalent of a television that's never turned off. Old grease, cigarettes, hair spray, pot, mildew, sweat, white rice, and sour milk played constantly. The rooms were small and dim, and they closed in on you. It was not surprising that so many of the kids living in the projects suffered from asthma.

Yet I wanted to be there. On the holy hill, Golgotha, the place of the skulls. I'd go months without visiting anyone in the projects, and then wake with a craving that was almost like physical hunger. I *missed* something, I *had* to be there. "To find the blessing that's been prepared for me," I said to Paul once.

"I know," he said.

Like certain people I was closest to, Paul believed in God. And what that meant for us had less to do with an intellectual stance or a creed, or even a well-developed sense of ethics and morality, the desire to "be good" or "do good." It was more like believing that the blessing prepared by God for us was everywhere, in the most unlikely places, for us to search out. And so of course we went everywhere, restlessly, looking for it.

Martha had found the blessing in her midforties slogging through anatomy class and late-night nursing rotations so that she could touch a diabetic's blackened leg or peer into the eyes of a stranger hit by a car. I found it by giving anyone who asked me something to eat. Paul found it all over the place, in the unexpected moments of wonder he noted whenever he stopped trying to be an "effective" priest.

Paul had complained when I asked him, the first time, to come anoint Laura in the projects, but he'd dressed for the occasion, in a long black cassock and a silver cross, and when he put his hands on Laura, wheezing in her sweatpants and tilting her damp face up for a blessing, he shivered.

"It was so inconvenient to go up there," Paul said to me later, "and then it turned out Jesus was waiting in that room."

Jesus really was waiting, in the different people around us, and we yearned to touch their bodies, just as the lame man and the leper and the hungry crowds had yearned to touch Jesus. If we touched them—even a little bit, even without understanding it all—we thought we could be healed.

The story goes that Jesus heads off to heal a sick girl, and on the way people come to announce that the girl has died already.

Don't be afraid, says Jesus, "The child is not dead but asleep." Don't be insane, say the people, dead is dead. The father weeps, the mother wails, everyone is distraught, but Jesus goes to the room of the little girl and takes her hand. "Little girl," he says, "get up." She gets right up and begins to move around. "Give her something to eat," says Jesus.

Give her something to eat, he says. Jesus keeps calling us to share in God's work of touching, healing, feeding, and mercy: not in some imaginary or theoretical way, but physically, in order that resurrection can happen.

I was hanging out in front of the pantry one afternoon, while people were waiting in line to get food. Suddenly someone started yelling: a woman was collapsing. I ran over. She was a small white woman with long hair, and she was seizing. Her eyes were rolling back in her head, and her knees were buckling, and her big, scared boyfriend was shouting.

I so did not want to be a part of this drama. I told someone to call 911 and went over and reached out my hand, and the woman grabbed me. She fell on me, clutching me and repeating, in a desperate, strangled voice, "I can't breathe." I took that as an encouraging sign, as people who really can't breathe generally don't have enough breath to say so.

But it took all my strength to hold her: she was terrified, and her body kept shaking as the seizures swept through her. "Oh, yeah, I see her all the time on Capp Street," a guy next to us said. "She must have got some bad dope." Great, I thought, now she's going to die right here.

Her eyes rolled back again, and I eased her down on the sidewalk and started stroking her forehead; then, out of nowhere, she began to croon her own name. "Lydia," she said. "Oh, Lydia."

It was as if she were remembering, very long ago, someone stroking her forehead and calling her into being by name. As if she were giving me and the strangers around her the very Word of her being, the spark in the darkness of her hurting flesh. As if she were asking me to receive her. As if she were Jesus, the Word that speaks its

146

own name and calls everyone else into being. Lydia, Jesus, Lydia: beloved child of God.

She sat up after a while, and one of our volunteers brought her a little cup of water. I went back inside when the kind, seen-it-all paramedics showed up, and later Lydia just lurched away on her own steam.

There are moments in each of our lives when we get to witness the truth. It doesn't always look beautiful. But it's so bright that you can stand there, with every little grungy detail lit up, and see the beating heart of the living God.

Will Hocker was used to being the person who said the unsayable thing: with infinite gentleness and a refusal to be rushed, he'd make room for scared, inarticulate families to talk together about death. It took discretion and patience. As he told his volunteer chaplains, it was important in terminal cases to help families discuss options, and to fill out legal forms ahead of time to ensure their wishes would be met. Dying was a complicated business in the American health care system, and denial usually resulted in last-minute chaos, confusion, regrets. He'd offered to come up to the projects with me, to see if he could help Laura sort through the details.

Laura didn't need much help.

"Father Will," she said firmly, "we've had our discussion, and Gabriel and Gloria agree. If I'm dying and can't breathe, I want the ambulance crews to resuscitate me; I want to go to the hospital so they can revive me. But I don't want to live unconscious on a machine if that's the only way I can stay breathing. We signed all the papers."

Gloria took a Do Not Resuscitate order out of a battered file folder, and handed it to him. *"Eso no se necesita,"* she said to me. "We don't need this one." She held up the Health Care Proxy appointing her as the medical decision maker if Laura were incapacitated. "That's the one," said Gabriel, who was translating for her.

"I can see you've talked," said Will. He looked surprised.

"Yes," said Laura. "And we prayed about it together. Let's pray again now." She adjusted her nasal tubes and took my hand, then Gloria's. We all stretched out our hands to each other, bending our heads in the little room.

"God," began Will, "look upon your human family with love. Hear our prayers."

"Help my mom," said Gabriel. He was standing up, in his socks, and I could see what a tall man he was going to be. "Help me and Gloria take care of her."

"Papa Dios," said Gloria, *"solo tu sabes. Confiamos en tí."*

I put my hand on the side of Laura's head and smoothed her hair.

"Thank you, God," said Laura. "Thanks for Gabriel, the best kid. Thanks for Gloria, my sister, my heart, I love her so much. Thanks for Sara and Father Will, and keep everyone safe. Please forgive me for anything I've done bad, and let me live as long as you decide I should live. God, thanks, and take care of my family."

Gloria gave a little sob. "Amen," said Will.

"Amen," I said.

"So Sara," Laura said, "I've got another paper I want you to look at. Gloria is going to be Gabriel's mother."

At the end of the Gospel of Luke, Jesus finally finds the thing he was so impatient for. He carries it, stumbling, up the hill, and hangs there as the sky darkens. And then, before he stops breathing, he turns to the shattered people around him and makes them into a new family: *Woman,* he says, to Mary, who bore him, *behold your son. Son,* he says to his beloved friend, *behold your mother.*

In the season of Laura's dying, California was wracked not only by the 2008 presidential contest but by Proposition 8, a more pointed attempt at defining family. The national election pitted the stigmatized, mixed-race child of a single mother and a foreigner against a standard-issue white man from a decent background. California's Proposition 8, which would outlaw same-sex marriage, pitted whores and lepers, the cast out and despised, the unnatural, the unlawful, sissies, faggots, drag queens, bulldykes, trannies, leather daddies, butch girls, queer boys, intersexed teenagers, lesbian mothers, and gay bishops against "normal" families.

It made me think a lot about Jesus, and the scary way he says he's come to destroy families and burn down the "natural" order. Talking about how he will set parents against children, daughter-in-law against mother-in-law, families against themselves, he says: *Do you think I've come to bring peace to the earth? No, I tell you, but rather division.*

What Jesus is burning up on that hill, of course, is the future of the world as seen in human terms. He is replacing it with the fire of the perpetual present: the fire of Christ, the fire of baptism through death. The fire of new creation. Even on the road to Jerusalem, heading into his death, Jesus is talking about burning down the whole damn house...and *Oh,* he says, *oh how I wish it were burning already.*

Back in the early 1970s, when I was Gabriel's age, the country had been on fire: the cities were burning; the streets were full of marchers and National Guardsmen; the country was convulsed by assassins, drugs, and riots. Everything was turning over: women left their husbands, young men defied the law and the elders, inmates took control of prisons, poor people refused to obey the cops, parents and children were at each other's throats. I was young and fiercely antiauthoritarian and had no sense at all. My favorite chant at the demonstrations—not today's stage-managed events, but the ones that wound up with tear gas and running with your heart in your mouth—was *Two, four, six, eight; smash the family, church, and state.*

I had absolutely no idea, back then, that this was Jesus' chant. That it would turn out to be such a fundamentally Christian thing to say. *Smash the family*—smash the relations of power between men and women, young and old. *Smash the church*—break the relations of power between an official priesthood and the people of God, between manipulators of mystery and its helpless objects. *Smash the state*—break the relations of power that owe their existence to official violence, destroy the armies of the empire, break the iron bars of the prison house.

I could just hear Jesus chanting this. Or, to quote another saying I grew up with: "Burn, baby, burn." *And how I wish,* says Jesus, *that the fire were already kindled.*

But by the time I heard Jesus' diatribe, the idea of toppling the church or state seemed so remote that it wasn't particularly threatening to Christians living in the American empire. It was family, the other locus of power Jesus said he yearned to destroy, that most people took personally.

And yet "profamily" Christians thought Jesus was on their side. In his name, they wanted to "focus on the family" or "protect marriage" or restore "family values." In his name, they wanted to make sure that the wrong people didn't get married or have kids. In the cold postmodern capitalist world, family to most people seemed like the only safe place. It was home, love, a minivan full of blond children. And it was threatened by people like me—the mere existence of my wife and child destabilized others' sense of belonging. It was threatened by Laura and

151

Gloria—a couple with mixed citizenship and no legal right to live together, claiming that they were a family, too.

But Jesus was not talking about the cozy, affective private household idolized by contemporary Christians. In Jesus' time, family ruled as much as the temple did, or the soldiers of the imperial army. Your very name, your identity, was determined by whose son or daughter you were. Your role in life was completely circumscribed by your position in the family. Your freedom as an individual was negligible inside the family and in the network of families that made up tribes and nations. The father ruled the mother, the mother-in-law ruled the daughter-in-law, the elder brother ruled the younger brother.

And central to the construction of family, of course, was who was outside it. Families existed—in fact, just as they do now—to define outsiders. Widows and orphans, illegitimate children—these people had no power, no authority, no place. They were not full humans, because they did not belong to a family.

Jesus just burns that sucker down.

It doesn't matter anymore, he says, that you're related by blood, by circumcision, by name, by property, by geographic boundaries. It doesn't matter if you're a Jew or a Greek, slave or free, male or female. We're all children of God: born naked, with no vestiges of family position or citizenship that we can carry into the kingdom. We are liberated from human rules about who belongs and who has power and who deserves to be part of a family.

You could have a virulent skin disease or be without a savings account or be crazy. You could be a girl. You could be an orphan or an illegitimate child. And yet you are part of Jesus' family, the one he makes again and again as he burns up the ones we create to keep others out.

Two, four, six, eight. God is good at making families. Two men and a baby, four illegal immigrants, a widow and an orphan, Gloria and Laura and Gabriel—God doesn't care who the state calls a family. Proposition 8 would pass, but God can make children for Abraham out of the very stones.

And so, that November, I took the papers Gloria handed me. Will called Caroline, an impatient, generous lawyer from St. Gregory's congregation, and got her to drive up to the projects one evening and sit next to the battered oxygen tank and notarize the letter.

"It doesn't really have full legal weight," Caroline said to Gloria, while I translated. "But you don't want to go to family court and try to do a full adoption. This will help protect Gabriel." She scratched Baby. "Cute dog," she said. She shook Gabriel's hand. "Glad to meet you," she said. She looked at Laura, and rose. "I'm honored to know you," she said. "Keep me in your prayers."

It would be one of the rare occasions where God's truth becomes the official record, and where the real family—made by following Jesus across the boundaries of convention—would become the official family.

153

"Ven, hijo," the undocumented foreigner would tell the illegitimate child. Come, child. At the foot of the cross, the mother would behold her son. And resurrection would begin.

✠

The last time I saw Laura alive, she was eating carrot sticks, propped up in a hospital bed. "I'm going home tomorrow," she announced. "I'm not going to die here." She was having trouble breathing, but I had no idea how close Laura might be to what she sometimes called "the other side." There were moments it seemed as if she could go on forever, the air rasping through her wrecked lungs, as she made endless arrangements by cell phone. "Gloria's getting a friend to come pick me up," she said. "So don't worry; I'll call you if we need anything."

I got the call around five-thirty in the morning, a couple of days later. "Sarita," said Gloria, her voice close and infinitely far. I heard her breathe, suspended in the space between sobbing and speech. "Sarita," she said again, "Laura has fallen. She's gone."

Everyone was outside when I arrived, the sky almost light and the air almost visibly blue. "Very early in the morning, on the first day," recounts the Gospel, "the women went to the tomb." There they were: three black women from the projects had bent themselves around Gloria, sheltering her, holding her. Gabriel was standing alone a few feet away, his face hidden in his sweatshirt hood, cradling Baby in his arms. I went over and grabbed him, and then Gloria grabbed both of us. We breathed.

"Come with me, Sarita," said Gloria. "Gabriel, wait here." There were two cops by the steps, one a scared rookie whose first dead body this was. I put on my best impersonation of nice-white-lady authority, and turned to the older cop, a petite woman listening to her radio and waiting for the medical examiner. "It's OK," I said, "I'm the pastor. We're not going to touch anything. I'm just going to go in with the family and pray."

Laura was inside, fallen, her great body wedged between a wall and the bed. Her skin was not yet stiff, and her eyes were closed. We knelt down to touch her, and Gloria poured out the story of Laura's last night on earth, how Laura had said she was sorry "if I ever said anything that hurt you," and then how the two women had lain together, until at three in the morning Gloria woke because Laura had stopped breathing.

"Depart, O Christian soul," begins the prayer appointed by the Book of Common Prayer for the time of death, "out of this world." There in the little room we made quick arrangements—Gloria had called Gabriel's father and the Pentecostal church elders, I'd call Will Hocker and the mortuary, I'd handle the cops—and I gazed at the corpse. "Lord," I said. "Lord, have mercy."

Will would whisper the rest of the prayer an hour later, as Gabriel lay on his mother's chest, sobbing, and Gloria bit her fist, and I held the little teacup of Wesson oil that I'd scavenged from their kitchen. "In the name of God who created you, Jesus who redeemed you, and the Holy Spirit who sanctifies you," Will would pray, dipping his thumb into the oil and anointing Laura's smooth forehead, "May your rest be this day in peace, and your home in Paradise."

There would be bustle in the now-crowded living room, as dawn broke and the comrades from AA began to arrive, along with the Agua Viva preacher in his pressed shirt, the church women in their long skirts, and some neighbors. "Our sister is with God," the preacher would tell everyone, in his soft Spanish. "She doesn't need us now. The most important thing we have to do is pray for this boy." Gabriel would mutely receive the hands of the preacher, as the little group clustered around him, calling on Jesus to lift him up. Gloria would make her last farewells, alone in the little room, murmuring and stroking the hair of the woman she loved. And then Will and the preacher and the visitors would leave, and Baby, worn out from all the company, would finally fall silent.

It was almost ten in the morning when we tried to raise Laura.

I'd sent Gabriel and Gloria over to drink coffee in a neighbor's apartment, so that the men from the mortuary and I could attempt to get the body onto a gurney. By now her bulk was even more solid, and there was less than a foot of room for us to stand in, between the bed and the body and the wall. The guys seemed to have no more idea than I did how to lift her up.

"Slide it under," the older white man said. But Laura's weight immediately broke one wheel of the gurney. His assistant, a younger, light-skinned black guy, sighed. Slowly, with gestures and quiet directions, the mortician directed us to roll and pull, push and lift, until most of the body was on the board. The straps weren't long enough, though, to bind her, so I began to tear strips from her bedsheets and wrap them, tenderly, around the body. "Tighter," said the mortician. He was balding, with an old-fashioned short-sleeved white shirt and big glasses. "The thing is, we're gonna have trouble getting her through the hallway, then you got the stairs, then outside the side-walk's got potholes, and I'm worried she could roll off."

I finished unhooking all the breathing tubes and the IV, and bound Laura's massive arms to her chest with the cloth. Her flesh was cool and smooth. The younger man gave up trying to fit the canvas body bag over her, and helped me with another set of sheets. We raised a leg. The room was close, but we worked quietly, calmly, without chattering or jokes. I pulled Laura's nightgown closed around her chest. "Let's try lifting again," said the mortician. "Raise, now."

There's so much gravity here on earth. We couldn't raise her. But with the help of strangers and scraps of her past, Laura's body was finally heaved onto the low wobbly gurney, and wheeled and pushed out the broken doors of her dwelling place, past her weeping and still breathing family, and hoisted into the waiting van.

The death of a beloved is an event that rings and rings through a life: bearing it is not a problem to be solved, but a long, slow piece of music to listen to. And mourning, like music, is best listened to with others.

"Hallelujah, praise God," sang a small, wiry guy from Agua Viva. "Jesus is risen; Jesus is here." He had plugged his guitar into a little amp with an extension cord, and was leading the music. About twenty Pentecostals joined in rather tunelessly on the choruses, as Will Hocker, in a black cassock, censed Laura's ashes. They rested on St. Gregory's altar, in front of a poster Gabriel had made on my computer, with a photo of his mother smiling, hair spilling over her neck. "Although we are apart," the poster read, "your spirit is with in me."

I'd never seen anyone actually thump a Bible before, but the pastor from Agua Viva did it enthusiastically, raising his hand in praise and calling for witnesses. He tore through some dire warnings from Revelation, made a few remarks about St. Paul and the importance of right living, and then asked if anyone would like to dedicate themselves to Christ "before it's too late."

I was pretty sure none of the members of St. Gregory's had ever imagined hosting a liturgy mixing Spanish altar calls with their beautiful chanted Byzantine prayers. I was having a hard time wrapping my own head around a stern immigrant pastor conducting a funeral for a gay woman alongside a bunch of drunks, some overeducated Anglicans, and a left-wing Jesus freak. But as I'd learned the night of the Candomblé service in Anibal's apartment: God loves what's from the heart. And our raggedy collection of mourners needed God to look on our unorthodox hearts with mercy, and bless us all.

A few of the AA guys took advantage of the preacher's invitation to come forward and testify. Mostly, they just wanted to talk about Laura. "She was a warrior," said a man named Hector. "She suffered a lot, but she had energy for everyone. She saved my life."

Yolanda, a black woman from the projects, jumped up and spoke in English, telling a long story about how she'd met the big woman with the little Chihuahua. "I'm one of Laura's homegirls," she said. "Now Gloria's my homegirl, too, and you, Gabriel, you're my homeboy." She sobbed.

Gabriel, in a tight black suit, gripped my hand tightly. "I really don't want to talk," he said, under his breath. "Oh

159

God, I don't want to have to say anything." But when the pastor called him forward he stood up straight. "Thank you all for coming," Gabriel said. "I miss my mom so much."

Everyone applauded. "One more," said the pastor.

"I used to go past her window every day," called out Yolanda's companion. He was an older black man, with a salt-and-pepper beard. "I'd say, 'Hey, Laura, I love you.' And she'd say, 'I love you, Pablito, and God does too.'" One of the Mexican guys was translating, and I saw a group of men nodding in approval. "I loved her, and she loved us, and she loved God," said Pablo. He took a deep breath. "That is all."

"Thank you," said Gloria. She was wearing new sneakers and a black sweater, and I thought of how she'd told me, before the funeral started, that Laura had held her tightly on the last night, and thanked her. "I've had a lot of lovers, Gloria," the dying woman said. "But you're the one." Gloria's voice was steady now, but there were tears running silently down her cheeks. Mark Dukes's great saints danced above us, the gold of their halos gleaming in the candlelight, and a couple of little kids inched closer to the card table set up with refreshments.

Gloria looked around the room, and Gabriel smiled at her, encouragingly. "At the hardest time," she said, her Spanish formal and slow, "there's always a word of hope."

The resurrection of Laura didn't depend, really, on what the pastor from Agua Viva shouted, or what I believed, or what any of us thought about an afterlife. "Your spirit is with in me," said Gabriel's misspelled, heartfelt poster, and that was, quite literally, the truth.

I could see Laura alive in Gabriel, as he twisted a piece of paper in his hand and rested his head, tenderly, on my shoulder. I could see Laura alive in Yolanda and the AA men whose lives she'd saved with her bossiness and generosity. I could see Laura alive in myself, as I received the gift of her family—a gift she'd handed to me, a stranger, to love. And I could see Laura alive in Gloria. In whose small, dark, unremarkable body she looked, uncannily, like Jesus.

"In Laura's name, I thank you for the lessons you gave to her, to me, and to each other," Gloria said. "Life is very short. What can we do? Well, love one another."

follow me

There's often a moment when I'm hanging out with a group of Christians—usually liberal Christians, the kind who care about global warming and inclusive language—and I see them glance at me as if I'm a total freak. I've embarrassed them by talking too much about Jesus. As if he were real.

Most Christians know so much more about the faith than I do. They grew up in Sunday School; they know their church's history and creeds by heart; some have even been to seminary and can read the Gospel in Greek. But when I tell them I met the risen Jesus in actual food, they often pull back a bit, as if I'd declared I saw the Virgin Mary on a tortilla. (Which, by the way, would make me very happy.) And when I tell them that Jesus said we can go ahead and heal the sick, that we don't have to wait for authorization from our bishops to raise the dead, they look worried.

It's like the point I used to reach with my secular friends and family, who were fine, intellectually, with the idea of religion. They were broad-minded and reasonable, and agreed there were lots of beautiful stories in the Bible. "But damn, Sara," said one, finally. "You *mean* this?"

I do mean it. I still can't fully explain who the Boyfriend is, but I see him at work everywhere, still breathing in all kinds of people: poor men, crazy women, middle-class retired couples, little kids. They're feeding, healing, forgiving, raising the dead.

It doesn't take that much to feed. You don't have to run a food pantry, like Michael, and serve eight hundred people a week. You could start a nonprofit restaurant, like Anthony and Karen, or, like Debbie, give peanut butter sandwiches to homeless guys in the park. Or you could just invite a stranger to dinner.

It doesn't take that much to heal. You don't need to change careers and become a nurse like Lawrence or Martha; you could volunteer as a chaplain like Cheryl. Or you could just tell an addict the truth about your own addiction, hug a friend instead of giving him advice, sit with a dying woman and not try to pretend.

It doesn't take that much to forgive. Well, to be honest, it does: it took me almost ten years to forgive someone who'd hurt me. But then one afternoon, unprepared, I just gave up: what the hell, I thought; I wish him happiness.

And raising the dead? This is what Christians do every Sunday, after all, when we stand around in our boring churches, eating little wafers or pieces of whole wheat pita, saying aloud that Christ is risen. It's what we do when-ever we continue in simple, literal acts: breaking bread, praying without hope of perfect outcomes, admitting our weaknesses, and loving people who don't deserve it. It's what we do when we remember that death is not the end.

A few months after Laura's funeral, I went to the camping goods store to buy some sunscreen, and after about fifteen minutes I left with one of those headaches I only get in the presence of too much consumer choice. On the first floor alone there were hundreds of different kinds of backpacks made of super-space-age bulletproof fabric with special zippers and pouches and solar water purifiers and GPS devices and headlights. I remembered how, when I was a kid, going camping meant we took a blanket to sleep in, and my dad maybe packed some marshmallows.

There seems to be an idea in the contemporary church that following Jesus requires a similar kind of outfitting and preparation. Apparently, Christians can't feed people without a permit from the state, a certificate from the church insurance fund, and a resolution at a denominational convention. You can't teach without audiovisual aids and rooms full of approved Christian gear. You can't touch sick people without 125 hours of supervised clinical instruction and latex gloves. You can't proclaim repentance unless you've been to seminary—and even then it's a bit dicey. And God forbid you should claim authority to act in Jesus' name without a feasibility study, a mission statement, a capital outlay of ten thousand dollars, and at least six months of committee meetings.

But ordinary people still hope, suspect, and believe they can be Jesus.

The formulas of religion may be so overfamiliar that many believers have a hard time acting as if this most surprising narrative is true. They may doubt themselves, and not understand why Jesus trusts *us* to do his work. They may be sick to death of the institution, tired of propping up a dysfunctional church, and trying to coast by without caring too much. They may, like me, be anxious because there's no way to be Jesus on your own private terms: you have to jump in and do it alongside your Boyfriend's other lovers.

But Jesus is real, and so, praise God, are we. Every single thing the resurrected Jesus does on earth he does through our bodies. You're fed, you're healed, you're forgiven, you're pronounced clean. You are loved, and you're raised from the dead.

Go and do likewise.

acknowledgments

M y whole life is inspired by the great love of Martha
Baer and Katie Miles, who feed, heal, and forgive me.
I give thanks.

The people of The Food Pantry and of St. Gregory
of Nyssa Episcopal Church continue to be a cloud of
witnesses sustaining me in so many ways. I'm grateful
to all of them, and especially to those who allowed
me to write about them, or to discuss parts of this
book: Maitreya Badami, Lynn Baird, Frances Baxley, Elizabeth Boileau, Nirmala Cadiz, Lawrence Chyall, Mark
Dukes, Paul Fromberg, Blanca Hansen, Steve Hassett,
Cheryl Hendrickson, Caroline Hinshaw, Will Hocker, Susan
Kellerman, Glen Leis, Tricia McCarthy, Mona Mejía, Virginia Miller, Matt Nichol, Michael Reid, Deb Tullman,
and Chris Viola. I've also been blessed to be part of a
larger community whose work is described in this book,
including Margaret Dyer-Chamberlain, Francisco Gonzalez,

AnneMarie Grace and the students of Downtown High School, Karen Leibowitz, the students and teachers of Live Oak School, Tricia McCarthy, Anibal Mejía, Anthony Myint, SOMA Area Ministry, Iglesia Torre Fuerte, Tree, and Debbie Little Wyman. I continue to draw strength from my beloved family and friends, from colleagues here and in food pantries and churches around the country, and from the strangers who've written to me, sharing the good news of their work.

I'm indebted to other Jesus freaks who read parts of this book and helped me think it through; and to those who talked with me about Christianity and worship, especially Nadia Bolz-Weber, Tom Brackett, Cláudio Carvalhaes, Sanford Dole, Rick Fabian, Paul Fromberg, Jeff Gaines, John Golenski, Anibal Mejía, Michael Plekon, Donald Schell, Jane Shaw, Daniel Simons, Phyllis Tickle, Philip Wickeri, and Dana Wright. I'm grateful that Doug Pagitt introduced me to Sheryl Fullerton, whose work as my editor can only be called a blessing.

For generously offering their homes and giving me space to write, I owe a great deal to Mark Pritchard and Cris Gutierrez, and to Jeff Gaines and John Griffin. Thanks also to Sean Swift and the staff at Bishops Ranch, whose openhearted hospitality made it possible for me to finish a first draft.

In memory of Laura, and for the living witness of her family, alleluia.

Sara Miles

Feast of the Transfiguration, 2009

For more information:

Sara Miles	www.saramiles.net
The Food Pantry	www.thefoodpantry.org
St. Gregory of Nyssa	www.saintgregorys.org
Episcopal Church	

the author

Sara Miles is the founder and director of The Food Pantry, and serves as Director of Ministry at St. Gregory of Nyssa Episcopal Church in San Francisco. Her other books include *Take This Bread: A Radical Conversion* and *How to Hack a Party Line: The Democrats and Silicon Valley*. Her writing has appeared in the *New York Times Magazine,* the *New Yorker,* and *Salon,* as well as on National Public Radio.